Personal Brand Creation in the Digital Age

Mateusz Grzesiak

Personal Brand Creation in the Digital Age

Theory, Research and Practice

Mateusz Grzesiak
Warsaw, Poland

ISBN 978-3-319-69696-6   ISBN 978-3-319-69697-3   (eBook)
https://doi.org/10.1007/978-3-319-69697-3

Library of Congress Control Number: 2017957652

Cover illustration: © Bitboxx.com

Printed on acid-free paper

This Palgrave Pivot imprint is published by Springer Nature
The registered company is Springer International Publishing AG
The registered company address is: Gewerbestrasse 11, 6330 Cham, Switzerland

CONTENTS

LIST OF FIGURES

LIST OF TABLES

CHAPTER 1

Introduction

Abstract This chapter sets out the issues addressed by this work and the approach to the topic of personal branding and YouTube. The main research questions and hypotheses are introduced, as are the research methods as well as the structure of the work.

Keywords Personal branding • YouTube • Social media

Over the past decade, from May 2005, when former PayPal employees Chad Hurley, Steve Chen and Jawed Karim released the first version of the YouTube service to the public, up until the present day, websites with short videos have ceased to play simply an entertainment role. Even though entertainment content continues to break records as the most popular, for some time now YouTube has been recognized as one of the most effective tools for exerting influence, shaping the taste of viewers and, what is most significant from the point of view of this work, shaping a personal image, in other words the phenomenon known as personal branding.

With each passing year, an ever-growing number of professionals, both individuals interested in building their own personal brand, as well as those who create images for products or organizations, are growing aware of the driving force that comes from competent and conscious use of the possibilities YouTube offers. The possibilities for the distribution of information

© The Author(s) 2018

M. Grzesiak, *Personal Brand Creation in the Digital Age*,

https://doi.org/10.1007/978-3-319-69697-3_1

and use of this dynamically developing medium for the shaping of a personal brand are indeed huge, for at least several reasons:

(a) free, wide access to content as well as the ability to publish for free
(b) low level of technical complexity
(c) ease of viewing
(d) international, trans-cultural and without broadcast limitations
(e) measurable penetration and scope of content distribution
(f) popularity of the service, providing a wide range of internauts with the ability to shape their personal brand.

There are many examples that show how the amount of funds invested in the production of videos for YouTube is not very important—often popularity records are set by material recorded using cell phones with an amateur soundtrack. It is the idea and the content of the published material that has the greatest influence on whether a video will "go viral" (viral ads—a trick used more and more often in advertising campaigns), and users themselves begin to distribute it, sharing it with their friends on their own YT channels or via the most popular social media such as Facebook or Twitter.

Today, amateur recording of video material practically does not require having either expensive equipment or specialized professional skills. The widespread development of cell phone providers offering smartphones as part of a subscription (the cost of which is "hidden" in the monthly subscription fee) has resulted in access to the ability to record video material becoming commonplace. Moreover, most amateur-level cameras, camcorders or even smartphones available on the marketplace today permit recording in high resolution (HD), with stabilization, editing and processing on the device itself (without the need for any specialized software).

Video material viewed by internet users does not require any interaction from them, no engagement or for them to do anything additional at all. A user does not need to actively participate in exploring such material, does not need to click on anything or scroll through screens to view the next items. Moreover, the run time of most video material on YouTube does not usually exceed a few minutes, which is a conscious decision on the part of creators to make maximal use of the first level of user interest and show content before the level of interest falls. This trait of the material on the YouTube service was noticed by specialists in sales and promotion—the short format sells much better, as users are more eager to view it.

The global reach of the internet as well as the fact that YouTube is not divided into dedicated domains for specific countries means that distribution of material is unlimited (Schwabel, 2010, p. 37). A video published in one place on the globe is available at the same moment for all users of the network. There is no limitation regarding the general time of the broadcast or the time of day. There or no limitations regarding the timeslot, television channel or station or its range. YouTube has global reach and makes it possible to open the materials it hosts in every corner of the world at any time.

A channel on YouTube offers huge opportunities for research. It makes statistical data available that contain a great amount of information, ranging from the demographic profile and localization of its users, through statistics regarding hits, views and subscriptions, on the basis of which one can easily determine the global reach of a given item of content published on the service. That alone attracts interest in the marketing opportunities of YouTube, which cannot be overestimated, from more and more companies and corporations (Malinowska-Parzydło, 2015, p. 226) that only just over a decade ago could not even dream of such an inexpensive promotional tool that at the same time operates worldwide.

Before the rise of YouTube, the tools available for shaping a personal brand were limited to operating in the public sphere using traditional media. However, presence in the traditional media, both for brands and for individuals, required overcoming a high financial barrier (purchase of paid advertising or entire promotional campaigns) and also the long-term process of becoming a public figure. This process often took years, and depended on a number of factors: media interest, talent in the given field, journalistic and acting ability, et cetera. The appearance of YouTube, together with its whole range of possibilities, not only made this process shorter, but also opened access to effective instruments for shaping a personal brand (Neher, 2013, p. 16). Today, personal branding tools are free (Malinowska-Parzydło, 2015, p. 74) and available to everyone (Schwabel, 2010, p. 7). The difference lies above all in the different terms of entry. For example, appearing on a television program is only possible when someone is invited to do so. Appearing on YouTube requires no invitation, and only the content determines how many viewers (sometimes millions of them) will become familiar with the performance (Montoya & Vandehey, 2008, p. 231).

The number of users of the service who decide to give up using traditional media such as broadcast or satellite television channels or local and national radio broadcasts is also growing. For them, YouTube is the primary medium for music and film distribution. The number of views received by the most popular YouTube channels exceed many times over the possibilities of the most popular television stations, and this of course attracts huge interest in the service from both advertisers and many companies seeking to recruit employees.

One of the premises of taking up the problem of personal branding in this work is the dependency, that is becoming clearer and clearer, between the opportunities for earning income from advertising or finding a lucrative occupation and a personal brand constructed using YouTube. This work addresses topics having to do with building and negotiating a personal brand, considering in particular the tools for shaping a personal brand on YouTube and the effects of using them professionally.

The main goal of this work is to identify and compare strategies for shaping personal brands used by young Polish and American internauts and YouTubers, which constitute examples of the success of personal branding and make it possible to establish a set of effective practices.

The work seeks answers to the following research questions:

- Is YouTube an effective tool for shaping a personal brand for members of the younger generation (Generation Y and Generation Z)?
- To what extent are YouTubers, who are building their image with the service, recognizable?
- How is YouTube perceived in regard to achieving financial success?
- What effect does a well-constructed personal brand have on finding work and getting to know new people?
- To what extent is the idea of a personal brand known?
- What social media do members of the young generation use?
- Do members of the young generation build a personal brand? Do they do so consciously?
- To what end do members of the young generation build a personal brand?
- How are the ways of building a personal brand different among members of the young generation in Poland and the United States?

The results of the empirical research, supported by the use of secondary data and references, have the goal of verifying the following research hypotheses:

Primary hypothesis: YouTube is one of the most effective tools for shaping a personal brand for members of the young generation.

Secondary hypothesis: Professional preparation of a personal brand on YouTube is becoming a passport to gaining a presence in the traditional media and to the receipt of advertising contracts.

Apart from a critical review of the literature on personal branding, the work also includes the results of the author's own research conducted using case studies based on in-depth interviews with selected Polish YouTubers (Red Lipstick Monster, Jaś Dąbrowski and Wapniak) as well as quantitative research conducted with an online questionnaire. This questionnaire consisted mainly of closed questions, which included questions using a scale (primarily a five-point Likert scale), cafeteria-style disjunctive and conjunctive questions as well as alternatives. The quantitative research was conducted in May 2016 among members of the young generation (18–34 years of age) in Poland and in the United States, who regularly use the Internet and social media. The sample size in Poland was 500 individuals, and 504 in the United States.

The structure of this work is as follows:

The first main chapter, Chap. 2, consists of a rough history of personal branding as well as how it is now conceived. It describes the goals, strategies and challenges related to personal branding in the contemporary, globalized world.

Chapter 3 characterizes the process of shaping a personal brand with an overview of the challenges posed by the information revolution. This chapter includes a comparison of traditional methods of shaping a personal brand and e-branding. It presents the characteristic traits of each strategy and places them into the broader context of generational differences among message recipients. It illustrates the marketing potential of the Internet with examples of effective e-branding campaigns.

Chapter 4 addresses the question of personal branding on YouTube, and constitutes an attempt at a comparative analysis of the ways this social medium is used to shape personal brands in Poland and in the United States. This chapter characterizes the cultural and technological conditions that determine personal branding strategies in each country, and the main ways in which shaping a personal brand is changing in Poland and in the United States.

The author's own empirical research is discussed in Chap. 5. The methodological assumptions of the research are characterized, including the research questions, goals and hypotheses, and the characteristics of the study group are given. The results of this research are presented in two parts: a qualitative one, based on case studies of recognized YouTubers in Poland, and a quantitative one, based on a questionnaire given to two groups of respondents (young Internet users in Poland and in the United States).

The last and sixth chapter offers interpretation of the results in regard to theory and the current state of the field, and also includes conclusions and recommendations for practice that emerge from the research.

REFERENCES

Malinowska-Parzydło, J. (2015). *Jesteś marką. Jak odnieść sukces i pozostać sobą.* Gliwice, Poland: One Press.

Montoya, P., & Vandehey, T. (2008). *The brand called you: Make your business stand out in a crowded marketplace.* New York: McGraw-Hill Education.

Neher, K. (2013). *Social media field guide: Discover the strategies, tactics and tools for successful social media marketing* (2nd ed.). Cincinnati, OH: Boot Camp Digital.

Schawbel, D. (2010). *Me 2.0, 4 steps to building your future.* New York: Kaplan Publishing.

CHAPTER 2

Personal Branding: Its Essence, Goals and Classification

Abstract This chapter consists of a rough history of personal branding as well as how it is now conceived. It describes the goals, strategies and challenges related to personal branding in the contemporary, globalized world.

Keywords Personal branding • History • Goals • Globalization

HISTORY OF PERSONAL BRANDING

The tradition of branding reaches back many centuries. The concept of *brand* comes from Old Norse, in which *brandr* meant "sword, fire, to burn." This term was used to describe the practice of marking products by burning the name or symbol of the producer into them (Ritson, 2006).

The oldest brand that still exists today has its origins in the Vedic period (ca. 1100–500 BCE). This is an herbal paste, *chyawanprash* (also spelled *chyavanaprasha*, *chyavanaprash*, *chyavanaprasam* or *chyawanaprash*), made using 49 different herbs, that is consumed for its healthy properties. Its formula was created on the edge of the crater of the Pahadi Dhusran volcano in northern India.

Roman glassmakers in around the first century CE marked their wares with their own trademark. The most famous of these was Ennion. To this day some of his glassware survives, bearing the Greek inscription "made by Ennion" or "Ennion made me" in a rectangular frame. Some vases have the added phrase "may the buyer be remembered", presumably "by the gods" (Johnson, 2015). In the thirteenth century in Italy, paper watermarks were used to mark products (Colapinto, 2011); the technique was first used by artisans in Fabriano in 1282 (Meggs, 1998, p. 58).

Yet these examples might be thought of as proto-brands, and the actual birth of a brand associated with a trademark came in the nineteenth century with the rise of distribution of packaged goods. Industrialization meant that the production of many household goods moved from local manufacturers to large centralized factories. Owing to the need to transport their goods, manufacturers marked their goods, placing their trademarks on packages, barrels or containers.

One of the first intentionally introduced trademarks is the logo of the British brewery, Bass & Company. The brewery's owners assert that their red triangle is the oldest trademark in the world, having been registered on January 1, 1876 (Bonigala, n.d.). The company Tyte & Lyle, however, also claims this title. Its best-known product, Lyle's Golden Syrup, was entered into the *Guinness Book of World* Records as the oldest brand in Great Britain, and its golden-green package has remained unchanged since 1855 (Hibbert, 2008). Another example comes from Ferentino, Italy; since 1731, the Antiche Fornaci Giorgi brickworks there has been marking all of the bricks it produces with a stamp, which comprises a sort of proto-logo. Their oldest examples are preserved in buildings in the Vatican (Storia della Fornaci Georgi, n.d.).

Cattle have been marked in a similar way for decades. This practice originated with Texas rancher Samuel Maverick, who came up with this as a solution to the problem of escaped cattle. A sign was branded into the animal's skin to make it easier to recognize who an animal belonged to when stray animals were found (Maverick, 1942, pp. 94–96).

The factories that arose in the course of the Industrial Revolution began to produce goods on a mass scale, as production by hand was replaced by machine production. Manufactured products reached a wide range of consumers, and not only locals who knew the brand. Simultaneously, packaging grew in importance, serving to break through the initial mistrust of consumers who did not yet know the manufacturer's goods. The creation of a solid, trustworthy brand became the path to building trust and customer loyalty. Pears Soap, Campbell's Soup, Coca-Cola, Juicy Fruit chewing gum or Quaker Oats were among the first brands that were consciously created so that consumers could identify with the values they represented, thereby building a relationship between the brand and their customers.

In 1900, James Walter Thompson published *The Thompson Red Book on Advertising*, in which he explained the role and significance of using a trademark in advertising. This was the first attempt to scientifically explain the significance of brands in a commercial context. Soon, firms began to invest greater resources in advertising: slogans, mascots and jingles began to appear on radio and later television, creating positive associations with a given brand. Producers came to realize that in this way they could build social and psychological relationships with customers.

Over the course of a dozen or so years, creators of brands focused on brand identity because they noticed that customers, when making their purchases, steered toward brands and the associations they had with them—for example, luxury, fun, practical—and not with the products themselves. This trend continues unabated and today it is possible to measure the value of a brand by comparing the expected revenues from a branded product with the expected revenues from a corresponding unbranded product. Naomi Klein calls this phenomenon brand equity mania (Klein, 2004). For example, in 1988, Philip Morris purchased the Kraft brand for a sum six times larger than its actual calculated value. This is a testimony to how customers, when buying a product, do not only consider its actual value, but also the value that is embedded in the brand itself.

The marketing campaigns of large international brands constantly focus on building brand image, which results in the growth of profits. Coca-Cola, in the second quarter of 2015, made $3.1 billion in net profit on gross revenues of $12.2 billion (Frączyk, 2015), after advertising expenditures were increased at the beginning of the year. In Poland, between January and May 2015, similarly to the previous year, the most advertised brand was Coca-Cola. Its marketing budget in this period was PLN 51.5 million, or as much as 82.3% higher than a year before ("Więciej reklam napojów", 2015). This was mostly an image campaign celebrating the 100th anniversary of the introduction of the legendary bottle.

The financial success of Coca-Cola is the effect of many years of consistent work building its image on the market. One only need remember that the company has been a strategic sponsor of the Olympic Games ("The Coca-Cola Company maintains", n.d.), and also supports many other sporting events, including football. It was Coca-Cola that was the first carbonated drink consumed in space. Since 1931, Coca-Cola has made advertisements every year with Santa Claus, which have become in many countries a sign of the approach of Christmas ("5 Things you never knew about Santa Claus", 2012). Coca-Cola shows the flexibility necessary for building trust: its logo is modified to the demands of the local market and written in the local manner, for example, in Chinese characters or Arabic script (Mooney, 2008).

Among clothing brands, the most valuable non-luxury brand today is Nike: last year its value was estimated at $30 billion. This is related to the image-building work by the American sports apparel powerhouse. Nike launched its #BetterForIt campaign, directed primarily toward women, with a view to raising awareness about the brand. Moreover, Nike constantly invests in its own training app Nike+ Running, which means that the brand has a presence in many areas of customers' lives (Kisiel, 2015).

Nike's marketing activities have been focused for years on building a particular image of the company among consumers. The first star Nike cooperated with was the then incredibly popular Michael Jordan. This was the first contract of its kind in the history of sports. Nike created a signature collection with the athlete's name, with an entire line of basketball shoes—Air Jordan. Other athletes who supported Nike with their names included Lance Armstrong, Andre Agassi, Michael Schumacher and Tiger Woods. Last year, the advertisement with football stars on the brand's Facebook page, which has over 15 million followers, received over 60 million views in a month. Currently, some of the best athletes in the world have advertising contracts with Nike, including Cristiano Ronaldo, Robert Lewandowski, Kobe Bryant, Wayne Rooney, Eden Hazard and Tim Howard (Szewczyk, 2014).

Personal Branding in Contemporary Marketing

The strategies used to build a commercial brand have begun to be used successfully for image building by people in the public sphere—politicians and actors, but also scientists and entrepreneurs. At first, emphasis was placed only on the benefits of direct contact with clients. In time, however, not only was the direct reflection of value in terms of profits recognized, but also the long-term benefits that emerge from building credibility in the eyes of clients.

This phenomenon was first noted by Napoleon Hill (2013 [1937]) in his book, *Think and Grow Rich*. This is when the link began to be made between financial results and the ability to convince people directly based on the image of the individual. Greater personal brand value translates into greater effectiveness in negotiations or directly into more sales of goods and services.

This concept was further developed in 1980 in *Positioning: The battle for your mind* by Al Ries and Jack Trout. Positioning here is understood as an intentional process of brand development, which not only yields immediate benefits, but also significant help in shaping a whole career.

Personal branding was popularized by Tom Peters. This American author and expert in management practice emphasized the creation of a well-considered image by managers, which would yield not only a growth in authority and better results, but would also allow them to climb the corporate ladder. The crowning achievement of his work was the book *Movers and Shakers: The 100 Most Influential Figures in Modern* Business (Peters, 2003).

But the real expansion in personal branding was made possible by the Internet, which gave rise to the need of managing one's online identity. Further development of personal branding came along with the rise of social media, which created great possibilities for the distribution of virtual identity and using it to sell products or generate income. Today, personal branding[1] is mainly associated with the effective use of the tools of the new media, with which everyone can be a broadcaster.

Personal branding is based on particular marketing strategies and practices:

(a) Advertising goods or services using a recognized name, for example large brand-image campaigns using celebrities. For example, in Poland, the face of ING Bank in Poland has been the well-known actor, Marek Kondrat. A few years ago, the largest advertising agency in the country could pay over PLN 900,000 (Makarenko, 2010), or ca. $225,000, a hefty sum in Poland. World-class brands eagerly use the images of known footballers like Cristiano Ronaldo (Cavanagh, 2010), Kaka (Thomas, 2009) and Leo Messi ("Tata Motors partners with the football legend", 2015), or actors such as Brad Pitt (Heritage, 2012), George Clooney (Snyder, 2015) and Julia Roberts (Fitzpatrick, 2012).

(b) The possibility of linking two known brands in order to reach a greater number of customers. This type of marketing alliance is known as co-branding (the use of two or more brands on one product), licensed brands (granting rights to use a brand on other objects, for example, for the production of gadgets with the logotype of a sports club by an outside company), or cross-marketing (the owners of a brand make efforts to promote a partner's brand) (Sznajder, 2012, p. 121).

(c) Storytelling, or the use of certain narrative structures to build a brand image—the narrative created engages the consumer and is more accessible than traditional advertising. The story is based on what sets a brand apart from the competition and encourages the consumer to take action, often drawing on his or her needs and desires. The consumer can easily share the story via social media.

(d) A set catalog of effective practices for building and selecting the form of the message—in social media, getting receivers engaged is key. Social media sites provide many tools for measuring engagement. On the basis of these results, a catalog of effective practices can be made. One such example is posting pictures on Facebook—HubSpot research has shown that pictures receive 53% more likes than ordinary posts with the same content (Corliss, 2012). It is also important to use various channels to distribute content. For example, pictures mainly having to do with lifestyle are published on Instagram. The limited ability to add text or links means that content there mostly can help with long-term image creation, without an effect on direct sales of services. There is a similar situation with Snapchat, on which brands communicate with consumers through pictures with captions or short videos. Display times are between 3 and 10 seconds, and so this tool also is not suited for more elaborate messages (Sornoso, 2015). Brands also use Twitter, on which mostly short-status updates are posted (a maximum of 140 characters) or links to longer texts. YouTube is a platform for uploading videos, but thanks to its social media functions (subscriptions, the ability to rapidly share material from other services), it is preferred by brands for current promotion. The most comprehensive service is Facebook, with over 1.5 billion active users in the third quarter of 2015 (Statista, 2015), which allows posting a wide range of content.

(e) Proper placement of content—eye-tracking research has shown ("Eyetracking w e-mail marketing", 2013) that people first pay attention to the title of an item (for example, an email) and a face in a picture if one is included. The tendency to withdraw from reading longer messages is also notable. This has to do with the accumulation of a large number of stimuli on the Internet, which Liu and Huang (2005) discuss in their work:

With an increasing amount of time spent reading electronic documents, a screen-based reading behavior is emerging. The screen-based reading behavior is characterized by more time spent on browsing and scanning, keyword spotting, one-time reading, non-linear reading, and reading more selectively, while less time is spent on in-depth reading, and concentrated reading. (pp. 700–712)

Following these rules gives a marketer the chance to achieve better results. In the context of personal branding, proper placement of the face is particularly important, because most viewers focus their attention on it, regardless of the medium.

(f) Personal branding tools are also widely used to strengthen an existing market position. This is done by companies that use personal branding to promote their brands (e.g. the Teekanne brand using the image of Polish ski jumper and Olympic medalist Adam Małysz), as well as politicians, who try to draw attention to existing trends and skillfully plan their promotional activity. An example of good and effective political positioning might be Barack Obama, President of the United States, who built his own image based on authenticity, self-confidence and references to common values (Rampersad, n.d.).

THE GOALS OF PERSONAL BRANDING

Shaping a personal brand is usually a conscious and targeted activity. It can serve several different goals in the following areas:

(a) **Politics**—a personal brand in politics is a tool for achieving certain results, among which the most important is winning voter support and consequently winning elections. An example of how having a clear personal brand can turn into support from voters might be the success of Arnold Schwarzenegger, who in 2003 ran for the office of governor of California and won. The recognizability of a personal brand in other fields (in this case, movies) helped him to reach his goals in politics as well. Arnold Schwarzenegger served two terms, until 2011 ("Arnold Schwarzenegger", n.d.). Politicians are eager to use the support of other recognizable people who support them with their own popularity and authority. An example of this might be Vladimir Putin bragging of his friendship with the popular French actor Gérard Depardieu, or Barack Obama having the public support of stars such as Bruce Springsteen, Beyoncé or George Clooney (Urzędowska, 2012).

(b) **Advertising**—marketing experts in advertising campaigns are happy to make use of recognized individuals whose support can be good for the brand. In this case, there is a peculiar transfer of the celebrity's fans to the brand, and perhaps access to new groups of consumers. The presence of a star in an advertising campaign should both reinforce the message and lend it greater credibility. An example of this in the Polish market may be actors and celebrities who advertise banks, for example, actor Marek Kondrat, who has lent his name to ING Bank Śląski for years, or performer Szymon Majewski, who took part in advertisements for PKO Bank Polski. Stars advertise just about every kind of product or service, from tea (the Teekanne campaign with Adam Małysz) (Budzich, 2011), through cat food (Eva Longoria in ads for Sheba) (Smolicki, n.d.) through luxury cars (Matthew McConaughey in an ad for the Lincoln MKX) ("Matthew McCanaughey w reklamie", n.d.) or Jürgen Klopp in an ad for the Opel Insignia) (Trusz, 2015).

(c) **Social activism**—the participation of known individuals in social activism has a similar effect as it does in advertising: it increases its reach and raises its credibility and attractiveness. Its effects are also reciprocal—participation in a social campaign may make the given personality's image more attractive. There are many such examples, like the model Joanna Krupa, who is active in the struggle for animal rights, taking part in activism against wearing natural fur ("Joanna Krupa: 'I'd rather go naked than wear fur' ", n.d.) or footballers (including Neymar, Roberto Carlos, Mario Balotelli or David Luiz), who joined in the fight against racism ("Piłkarze jedzą banany!", 2014). Polish actors, including Wojciech Zieliński, Katarzyna Herman and Piotr Garlicki took part in a campaign against homophobia (Kucharski, 2013), and Joanna Brodzik, Michał Żebrowski, Tomasz Kammel, Hubert Urbański and Michał Szpak were part of the "*Nie czytaj!* [Don't read!]" campaign to promote reading ("Polskie gwiazdy mówią 'nie czytaj'", 2012).

(d) **Recruitment**—managers with high reputations in their environment, with a recognized brand built, for example, through activity on specialized social media such as LinkedIn or presence in the media, can more effectively attract people eager to work for them than the image of the company itself. Potential employees know that they will benefit from the abilities and knowledge of the given individual. Their presence in the public sphere makes candidates feel that they know their employer/supervisor better.

(e) **Finding work**—creating a consistent concept of one's own personal brand and creating an image online is one of the things required to find satisfying work. At the same time, research has shown that only just over half of all people look after their online image and do not post compromising pictures or comments, and 17% use only pseudonyms for online communication. Only one in three of those studied (34%) believe that search engine results can help in finding a better job and in professional development. Nearly half (45%) believe that their online image has no influence on their chances of finding employment. Only one Internet user in five (21%) sees the dangers of a negative image online ("Wizerunek w internecie a szukanie pracy", 2011).

(f) **Finding a partner**—a good personal brand enables a person to make a better first impression and consciously create their image, which makes them more attractive and increases their chances of finding a partner. As Dan Schawbel writes in *Me 2.0. 4 Steps to building your future*:

When you're trying to entice your friends to go to a movie or grab a drink at a bar, you're trying to sell an idea. You are using your sales skills and brand leverage to convince others to follow you – and you're being judged based on your approach. Each romantic encounter you have is, with all due respect, a selling proposition – from the first conversation to the moment a relationship is agreed upon, you are working to assure another that he or she is making the right choice. (Schawbel, 2010, p. 47)

(g) **Raising funds for charities and foundations**—the success of endeavors such as the Great Orchestra of Christmas Charity [*Wielka Orkiestra Świątecznej Pomocy*], Polish Humanitarian Action [PAH – *Polska Akcja Humanitarna*] or the Noble Box Project [*Szlachetna Paczka*] is linked with the charismatic figures who head the respective organizations: Jurek Owsiak, Janina Ochojska, and the Rev. Jacek Stryczek. Their clear images, as modest people, dedicated to the cause, not caring about privilege, luxury items or even their appearance (a t-shirt or yellow shirt in the case of Owsiak, Ochojska's fleece and sweaters, or the black clothing of Fr. Stryczek), make the message more credible and result in people being more eager to donate funds to the cause.

(h) **Building a business reputation**—personal branding can be an effective tool for building a reputation as a reliable person to do business with. This is particularly important in industries where the owner of the firm is generally also its public face and the enterprises' goods or services are promoted through this image.[2] An example of this might be trainer Randy Gage who, thanks to his image and consistent narrative of "from zero to millionaire", today successfully sells his books, training seminars and consulting services. Others earn through appropriate image management, including actors, who aside from their presence on television are often engaged in active participation in other areas of the public sphere—they manage their social media profiles, write blogs or appear in the media as experts. This builds their popularity, which is key for their profession, but also allows them to build their business image offstage. Journalists also are not content to create material only at their workplaces. They create blogs and videoblogs, communicate with readers on social media, position themselves as experts in concrete areas or as specialists in communication.

(i) **Promotion of cities, countries and regions**—in the promotion of particular locales, images of popular people are used, who are associated with the place or come from there. An example here might be the actor John Malkovich, who spoke in an interview about why it is worth retiring to Portugal (Fidalgo, 2014), or Eminem, who supported the candidacy of his native city, Detroit, in the competition for the NCAA Finals ("Eminem reklamuje swoje rodzinne miasto", 2009).

(j) **Reputation migration**—one brand may lend its reputation to another, an example of which might be the move made by Magda Gessler. The well-known Polish restauranteur, associated with good food and respected restaurants bearing her name, owns only a small share of these. Of twenty branded restaurants bearing her name, only three belong to her ("Licencja Gessler – jak ona to robi", 2007). Another example of the phenomenon, this time from the political arena, might be the support for the candidate for president of Katowice, Marcin Krupa, from the outgoing president Piotr Uszok in local elections in 2014. Uszok enjoyed tremendous social support among residents, but decided against running for re-election.

Instead, he supported the candidacy of his then deputy, Marcin Krupa, who in the end won the election (Pawlenka, 2014).

(k) **Lending personal qualities to fictional characters**—the good brands of well-known people are used, for example, by the creators of animated films. An example of this might be the strategy taken by the creators of the animated film *Shrek*. When casting voice actors, they chose easily recognized Hollywood actors, who brought the fictional characters to life not just with their voices, but also with features of their appearance and personality, through which the film characters became personifications of their personal brands. (For example, the on-screen Donkey was the reflection of Eddie Murphy, and Puss in Boots, Antonio Banderas). The creators of the Polish dubbed version did something similar, casting such well-known actors as Jerzy Stuhr and Zbigniew Zamachowski.

(l) **Brand ambassadors**—brands often use the services of well-known individuals in order to support the brand with the image of a celebrity or a known authority. In return for financial and/or material compensation, the ambassador agrees to use the brand's products or services. An example of this might be Mercedes-Benz, which with some to-do lent a car to well-known Polish author Szczepan Twardoch, free of charge. That was enough to provoke a national discussion about the writer's ethos, professional ethics and the commercialization of culture in general. It was not insignificant that Twardoch, one of the most recognized Polish writers, is in terms of image a good fit for a premium brand like Mercedes-Benz (Kiszluk & Nowacki, 2015).

Ways of Shaping a Personal Brand

Shaping of a personal brand can be divided into two types—employer branding and personal branding. Employer branding is shaping the personal brand of an employer with a view toward employees. Internal employer branding is directed toward current employees (and also to business partners and suppliers) and is intended to impart the system of corporate values, as to be able to deliver goods or services based on these values, which should as a result translate into customer satisfaction. External employer branding is directed toward potential employees and is intended to convince them that the given workplace represents the values they expect. In addition, external employer branding increases the number of applications an employer receives and improves their quality (Foster, Punjaisri, & Cheng, 2010, pp. 401–409).

Personal branding is constructing a personal brand through conscious image management. The most important determinant of personal branding is image personalization, which stipulates that the brand is the given person—"me" becomes the brand itself. The strength of a personal brand is built on the credibility of a real person and trust in them. An important characteristic of personal branding is also self-presentation (the content of the message is the person created for the brand, their strengths, interests, goals, passions, aspirations and so on) and the resulting narrative character of the message (storytelling is an inseparable part of personal branding—in building our own brand, we tell about ourselves).

Storytelling

According to the definition provided by the American National Storytelling Network, storytelling is the art of telling a story in such a way as to provoke a specific reaction in the listener. Storytelling is an interactive story, which forms the base for interaction between the teller and the listener (or group of listeners). The role of the storyteller is to actively create in the listener's mind a living image that stimulates the senses, presenting the actions of certain characters taking part in various events. Thanks to appropriate work by the teller, the story takes place in the senses of each listener. As a result, the listener becomes a co-creator of the story ("What is storytelling?", n.d.).

Stories inspire the imagination much more than dry figures do, so they are quite useful in the process of constructing a personal image or a sales narrative. Studies have shown that storytelling significantly increases the effectiveness of advertising. Research has also demonstrated that the human brain is not adapted to remembering facts. Students who listened to a one-minute speech filled with facts and narration remembered the story (63%) much better than the facts (5%) (Rush, 2014). It is for this very reason that storytelling is such an important and widely used tool in marketing.

Storytelling is used above all as a tool in sales narratives, in which the way that a product or service is presented is a story related to the desires, needs or the values of the customer. An example of a sales narrative might be the advertisement for Johnny Walker whisky—'Johnnie Walker. The Man Who Walked Around the World' (Fedczyszyn, 2014). In the case of personal branding, storytelling is a basic tool for image building. An example of an effective storyteller might be Polish designer Jacek Kłosiński, author of the blog *Blog dla kreatywnych* [Blog for creative people] (Kłosiński, n.d.). Thanks to well thought-out promotion, he gained over ten thousand followers on Facebook and has received invitations to numerous conferences as an expert in creative fields.

Brand Visualization

Just as storytelling places the emphasis on a story told with words, visual elements of branding should provoke the intended reaction, using certain symbols. For example, attire constitutes a key element of Jurek Owsiak's image, a man who always appears in public with glasses with heavy red frames. A characteristic element of the image of the band Gorillaz are their videos (and their entire visual identification) using the conventions of comics. Frequently, existing brands are strengthened by associations with famous people (icons)—an example might be the Nike Air series signed by Michael Jordan, the famous American basketball star. A similar scheme was used in the film *Shark Tale*, in which one of the main characters is reminiscent of Angelina Jolie. Both sides benefited from this, as the film's producers subtly brought the movie star into the animated film, and Angelina Jolie gained popularity among a new group of viewers (young audiences).

BRANDS AS A SUGGESTIVE AND COHERENT MARKETING MEDIUM

The elements of a brand are a collection of "hard" and "soft" cognitive elements, which together create its image. The test of the ability of brand elements to create associations lies in checking what consumers would think about a product if they knew only its name, logo, packaging and other brand elements.

A brand can consist of the following "hard" elements:

(a) Brand name—this may contain elements suggesting associations which are part of the brand image, for example, suggestions having to do with the consumer (the monthly magazine, *Twój Styl* [Your Style]), the content (the Herbapol[3] tea brand), or the situation for use of the product (APAP Night). This is not necessary, however—a brand name does not have to mean anything in particular to the consumer (Reebok, Agfa, Bosch). Its role may be limited to being easy for consumers to remember and distinguishing the product from others.

(b) Logotype—may, but does not have to suggest elements of brand image. The role of a logotype may be limited to making remembering the brand easier.

(c) Advertising slogan—this is a short sentence designed to raise brand awareness. It helps consumers to understand what a brand is, what its traits are and what makes it exceptional. (For example, the grocery store chain Biedronka: "*Codziennie niskie ceny* [low prices, every day]"; Leroy Merlin: "*Dla domu z pomysłem* [For home, with creativity]"), and supports identification with the values of the brand (for example, Opel: "*Wir leben Autos* [We live cars]"; Nike: "Just do it").

(d) Distribution channel—the channel by which a product reaches a potential consumer.

A personal brand is also made up of the following "hard" elements:

(a) Name—this does not does not always have to be a first and last name; many people over the course of their careers assume pseudonyms (for example, Lady Gaga, Prince), use a particular variant of their first and last name (for example, Kuba Wojewódzki, Kazik Staszewski[4]) or change their name (for example, Borys Szyc/Borys Michalak or Woody Allen/Allen Stewart Konigsberg).

(b) Logo—personalities who lend their names to a company, often have their own logotype (for example, Tony Robbins, Magda Gessler).

(c) Slogan—in the case of individuals, this is the phrase or formulation they say regularly and most frequently, so that it becomes their trademark (for example, journalist Mariusz Max Kolonko, "*Mówię, jak jest* [Telling it like it is]"; bodybuilder Robert Burneika: "*Nie ma lipy* [No bull]").

(d) Distribution channel—the medium, by which someone reaches their audience; this may be direct contact (for example, politician Janusz Korwin-Mikke), radio (for example, music journalist Wojciech Mann), television (for example, entertainer Kuba Wojewódzki) or the Internet (for example, independent filmmaker Sylwester Wardęga).

A personal brand is also made up of "soft" elements. These include:

(a) Behavior that is characteristic for the given person that sets them apart from others—for example, Usain Bolt and his victory gesture, Steve Jobs' way of walking, journalist Elżbieta Jaworowicz's way of sitting, or the theatrical stride of Angus Young of AC/DC.

(b) A person's way of speaking—especially elements that are typical for them, such as speed of delivery (for example, Jurek Owsiak at the finale of the Great Orchestra of Christmas Charity), accent (for example, Mongolian-born entertainer Bilguun Ariunbaatar), intonation (for example, psychiatrist Professor Zbigniew Lew-Starowicz), use of characteristic words (for example, Wojciech Mann), or a cultivated manner of speaking (for example, journalist and culinary critic Robert Makłowicz).

(c) Attire—the entire appearance or particular accessories that are typical for the given person and clearly associated with them. An example of this kind of accessory might be psychologist Krystyna Popiołek's hats, John Lennon's glasses, or Janusz Korwin-Mikke's bow tie. The entire characteristic way of dressing set apart Steve Jobs, for example, who at every new product presentation wore the same turtleneck and jeans. Similarly, Mark Zuckerberg always appears in a grey short-sleeved t-shirt.

(d) Appearance—although appearance is something unique in and of itself, certain elements (the shape of individual body parts) can become a calling card for a person and become associated only with them. Examples could be the mustaches of Salvador Dali or Adolf Hitler, Jennifer Lopez's or Kim Kardashian's buttocks, theater critic Maciej Nowak's hair, or the excess weight of the Grycan sisters.[5]

(e) Views—these can be the touchpoint for others to identify with the personal brand, and thereby also stand out from others. Examples could be Janusz Korwin-Mikke or musician turned politician Paweł Kukiz, who made their views part of their image

(f) Surroundings—people with whom a given brand is associated (for example, Cristiano Ronaldo surrounded by models), or places where they can be met (for example, parties with glamor model Natalia Siwiec or online personality Łukasz Jakóbiak).

(g) Props—objects that are unambiguously associated with a given person, making up part of their image, for example, Lech Wałęsa's oversized pen, politician Waldemar Pawlak's PDA, or Paris Hilton's dog.

(h) Self-awareness—being convinced of one's own value and life goals.
(i) Enemies—also issues, people or phenomena against which or whom the person fights, can become an element of their image, for example, model Joanna Krupa is associated with the fight against the killing of animals, actor Krzysztof Pieczyński against the Roman Catholic Church, and journalist Jakub Wątły with the struggle against various systems.

Levels of Awareness of the Existence of a Personal Brand

Brand awareness is one of the most important parameters of brand management, reflecting its state in the awareness of customers. It shows a customer's desire and readiness to buy a product of a specific brand, which constitutes a kind of cognitive simplification. It is also a strategy applied by consumers that allows them to save the time that would be needed to compare one brand with another. This strategy can help in choosing an offer of a specific brand (for example, the decision to subscribe to a particular YouTube channel), and in the case of the consumer goods market, to make appropriate purchases using cognitive simplification (Koniewski, 2012).

Three levels of brand awareness can be distinguished:

(a) **TOMA—top-of-mind awareness**—this is a brand that is best remembered and recalled, and so one which a customer independently chooses first (Koniewski, 2012). The greatest value is ascribed to this brand, because it is the first one considered when making a purchasing decision. The value of a TOMA brand, expressed in percentages, tells what percent of respondents regard a specified brand as first when making a purchasing decision for a given product (Lontos, 2009).
(b) **UBA—unaided brand awareness, SBA—spontaneous brand awareness**—these brands are indicated by customers independently, reflecting their range of choice, and thus their familiarity with the brands of the entire product category. This range is usually several or a dozen or so brands that are considered when making a purchasing decision. Top-of-mind brands are part of this range as well (Nurska, 2012).
(c) **Aided awareness**—if the customer is asked about a given product category, they are not able to name any brands, and only when they

receive a list of brands can they recognize a few of them. Brands that are known when seen or heard about belong to this category. Aided awareness is a sign of weak consumer ties to the given brand.

CHALLENGES FOR PERSONAL BRANDING IN THE ERA OF GLOBALIZATION

Numerous studies in the area of culturally conditioned financial decisions prove that investors from different geographical regions and different cultures, despite having many traits in common, make different investing decisions and approach such issues as risk differently (Breuer & Quinten, 2009, pp. 6–7). Management practice delivers many examples of setbacks in international companies that arose from cultural differences. The cultural factor may in fact be an important determinant of success or failure in the activities of an international company.

Culture is understood as "everything that people think do, and possess as members of a society" (Sztompka, 2002, p. 233). This notion refers to many aspects of life and thus one can speak, for example, of the culture of propriety, cultured speech or national culture. Geert Hofstede defines national culture as the "collective programming of the mind" of people who belong to a particular nationality. They share a national character, which is the representation of their "cultural programming." This character shapes values, assumptions, abilities and behaviors. Hofstede counts among the basic levels of this programming national culture, regional groups, gender, generational groups, social class and organizational culture (Hofstede & Hofstede, 1997, p. 17). Organizational culture is a collection of norms, assumptions, convictions and values as well as principles that constitute the fundamental model of behavior for a member of a given organization (Listwan, 2005, p. 75).

Hofstede points to the important difference between national culture and organizational culture. National culture is a part of mental programming that is acquired in the first decades of life, whereas we confront organizational culture at the threshold of adulthood or after entering it, when our values are already defined (Hofstede & Hofstede, 1997, p. 299).

Hofstede's Cultural Model

In the 1960s and 1970s, Geert Hofstede studied the behavior of IBM employees in over 70 countries around the world. On the basis of

116,000 completed questionnaires regarding the values that managers took a stance on, it was possible to distinguish the cultural dimensions of differences appearing between cultures. These dimensions allowed cultures to be compared and their characteristic traits to be described.

Hofstede distinguished six dimensions (Czerwonka, 2015):

(a) **Power Distance Index—PDI**—describes the relationship between supervisors and their employees, or on the national scale between the authorities and citizens; it also describes the level of acceptance of social inequality, the level of authoritarianism or the level of expected obedience.

(b) **Individualism vs. Collectivism—IDV**—shows the proportion between the weight placed on the good of the individual and of the group. Most societies are collectivist societies, in which the position of the individual is defined by belonging to a group; in a few individualistic societies, the position of the individual is determined by their own attributes.

(c) **Masculinity vs. Femininity—MAS**—indicates differentiated gender roles. In every culture, the feminine role includes care for the area of feelings and the preservation of harmony, and the masculine role assertiveness and aggressiveness. In feminine cultures, the behaviors of both genders are similar and tend toward the feminine pole, whereas in masculine cultures the differences between gender roles is greater, while at the same time the behaviors of both genders are closer to the masculine pole than in feminine cultures.

(d) **Uncertainty Avoidance Index—UAI**—describes the degree to which people are inclined to accept unpredictability in social relations and uncertain futures. A high uncertainty avoidance index is associated with, among other things, a high level of anxiety, public display of emotion and high alcohol consumption.

(e) **Long Term Orientation vs. Short Term Normative Orientation—LTO**—describes the development of virtues that bear fruit in the future, for example, tenacity or thrift. Short-term orientation entails cultivating virtues linked with the past and the present, such as a social emphasis on consumption.

Gesteland's Model

Richard Gesteland of the Copenhagen Business School, worked for decades in international corporations and created the model he calls "the great divide between business cultures", which, like Hofstede's model, describes types of business cultures.

He distinguishes the following cultures (Gesteland, 2005):

(a) deal focused vs. relationship-focused
(b) informal vs. formal
(c) monochronic vs. polychronic
(d) expressive vs. reserved.

Deal-focused cultures are characterized by an emphasis on meeting goals and completing tasks as well as reaching concrete results, whereas relationship-focused cultures are oriented toward building long-term friendly relationships built on mutual trust.

The dimension dividing cultures into formal and informal is similar to the power distance dimension in Hofstede's model. In formal cultures, great weight is placed on protocols, etiquette, social status and showing respect to individuals in high positions. On the other hand, members of informal cultures have a negative attitude toward rituals that emphasize status, deeming them incompatible with egalitarianism.

Time plays a very important role in monochronic cultures: deadlines and meeting them matter, as do punctuality, schedules and keeping to them. In polychronic cultures, time is perceived as being more flexible: less importance is placed on fixed deadlines or schedules, but rather relationships between people are more important than meeting deadlines at all cost.

Characteristic for expressive cultures is how people communicate in a manner that is much more emotional than do people from countries considered to be reserved. They use body language more frequently and more intensively, which for members of reserved cultures is unacceptable, and sometimes may even frighten them (Simpson, 2012, pp. 602–604).

In regard to the area of building a brand, the models above clearly indicate how essential intercultural communication is in the case of brands with a presence in various markets in various countries. Keeping this in mind, we can discern brands that are effective on a regional level, but have no power to act globally (for example, the singer Doda is highly recognized in Poland, but not around the world, or Natalia Janoszek, who is a Bollywood star, despite not being a popular star in her native country).

The following factors have an influence on whether a brand can break out of the regional level:

(a) knowledge of language (for example, Russian duet t.A.T.u. and Lithuanian band Brainstorm reached international listeners because they began to also record works in English)
(b) distribution channel (electronic media provide nearly unlimited possibilities to reach an audience, which is why the video interviews by Łukasz Jakóbiak, for example, are viewed around the world)
(c) message type (not using spoken language, for example, Sylwester Wardęga or Mr. Bean)
(d) topics (local, that restrict the possibilities of reaching wider audiences, for example, cabaret sketches or political questions; global topics are based, for example, on a universal sense of humor).

STRATEGIES FOR SHAPING A PERSONAL BRAND WITHIN THE CONTEXT OF GLOBALIZATION

We may consider different ways of transmitting a message when creating a brand within the context of globalization; what is important is to do so consciously. We can create a brand for local customers, taking into account the peculiarities of the local market. An example of this is certainly Kazik, a musician who sings about Polish politics, local peculiarities, malaise and problems, emphasizing things that do not work properly. A similar approach is taken by every Polish band singing in Polish. Among television personalities, Wojciech Cejrowski might serve as an example, who in his political journalism only addresses topics related to Polish realities, as opposed to Mariusz Max Kolonko, who speaks about various topics without any orientation toward a particular region or country.

Strategies for reaching a target audience may be conducted through the choice of appropriate language, topics or references to particular metaphors that are understood only in a small local context. Examples include film metaphors (for example, references to the films of Stanisław Barei), or a peculiar sense of humor familiar to a local audience. Silesian audiences are shown sketches of the cabaret troupe *Kabaret Młodych Panów* [Cabaret of Young Gentlemen] ("*Komunia* [Communion]" or "*W kopalni* [In the mine]") and also television programs by chef Remigiusz Rączka, who speaks Silesian when cooking. Jokes might also only be understandable by local audiences, for example, controversial on-air jokes by Kuba Wojewódzki and Michał Figurski about Ukrainian women.

A conscious choice of the target audience of branding takes place in the case of an advertisement that is limited in reach to a particular geographical area. This can be clearly seen in the example of elections, in which politicians mainly campaign only where their potential voters live (this is particularly evident in local elections). Local branding occurs when messages are formulated that address regional history. The sender then plays the role of a local ambassador. An example might be entrepreneur Rafał Brzoska, who emphasizes his origins in a Silesian village called Nędza. The Rev. Professor Józef Tischner often emphasized his highlander roots, footballer Robert Lewandowski shows his Polishness, and NBA player Marcin Gortat speaks openly about his country. Pope John Paul II in his statements often referred to his family and past in Poland, reminiscing about the local *kremówki* pastries from his hometown of Wadowice, evoking local patriotism and a sense of pride. In this way, one can strengthen an existing personal brand and expand its local reach.

One can also reach a position on the local market through characteristic objects. For example, in Ecuador Wojciech Cejrowski drank yerba mate and referred to local pride, earning respect and recognition at the local level. In a similar way, actor Steven Seagal uses attributes that are characteristic of cultures of the East, such as wearing a mandarin collar shirt or other elements of local clothing. This forms a link with the local audience and builds the brand with an image expected by that audience. The local audience, seeing a Western person dressed in elements of Eastern clothing, feels proud. For the same reason, Donald Tusk was photographed wearing a traditional hat in Peru.

We can also create brands taking on a global strategy that takes local conditions into consideration. These include:

(a) a micro-macro brand creation strategy—operating simultaneously on a local market, referring to local patriotism and traditions, and on the global market with references to one's own representation of the local market. An example of such a strategy might be Sean Connery, who always wears a kilt when in Scotland. In this way, on the one hand he builds his local image—Scots are proud that he represents them in the world and remembers where he is from—and on the other he is recognized the world over as Scottish.

(b) A local strategy showing adaptation to local markets at the global level—here we can distinguish two kinds of behavior: exposing expectations and adapting to them (for example, the band Genesis, which greets fans at concerts in every country in their language and adapts video material in such a way that fans can buy the version for their own country; disco polo band Bayer Full, who in concerts in China sing in Chinese; or AC/DC member Angus Young, who in concerts wears pants with the flag of the country he is performing in). It also means avoiding that which is undesirable in a given place—an example might be Princess Kate, who when visiting a mosque wore a head covering. In contrast, Michelle Obama did not wear a scarf during a visit to Saudi Arabia, which provoked a diplomatic scandal.

(c) A strategy of creating a personal brand using national or local brands—referring to one's origins (for example, Woody Allen emphasizing that he is a New Yorker), emphasizing national traits with positive overtones (Usain Bolt, who explains in an interview that Jamaicans train world champions, which is why his origins matter [Majendie, 2015]), use of set stereotypes regarding a given nationality (Pascal Brodnicki, whose culinary program enjoys great popularity, because according to Poles, the French know how to cook better than they do).

Another kind of strategy for building a personal brand is using another strong brand for this purpose. This can be done by using another personal brand, for example, through recommendations on book covers, mentioning someone's teacher (cardiac surgeon Professor Andrzej Bochenek emphasizes that he was the best student of Professor Zbigniew Religa, who performed the first heart transplant in Poland, or politician Ryszard Petru, who emphasizes that he was a student of Leszek Balcerowicz), or by the use of another non-personal brand, for example, through identification with a university or workplace (actor Jerzy Stuhr making references to the Krakow Academy for the Dramatic Arts brand, Natalia Lesz pointing to her acting studies in New York, or culinary journalist Maria Przybyszewska, who emphasizes that she worked as an intern in the best restaurant in the world, noma in Denmark).

The last type of strategy is a global strategy based on a message which is understood the same way in every culture. These are all the ways of creating a brand that refers to universal models, understood in all cultures regardless of origins, language or traditions. An example of this might be the candidates for the title of Miss World, who speak on stage about the need to fight poverty or the need to achieve peace in the world.

NOTES

1. In this work, personal branding, creating and shaping a personal brand are regarded as synonymous.
2. Building a strong business reputation and good relations with clients is an important factor in the growth of company value. For more, see Rudawska (2008).
3. Translator's note: a compound name consisting of two words—*herbata* (Polish for tea, also playing on the herbal association via Latin) and *pol*, short for *polska* or Polish, thus *herbata+polska* = Polish tea, also herbal/medicinal products.
4. Translator's note: each of these first names are diminutive or familiar forms, Kuba of Jakub, and Kazik of Kazimierz.
5. Translator's note: the Grycan sisters have a kind of celebrity status, and are the daughters of an important ice-cream producer in Poland.

REFERENCES

5 things you never knew about Santa Claus and Coca-Cola. (2012). Retrieved from http://www.coca-colacompany.com/stories/coke-lore-santa-claus

Arnold Schwarzenegger. (n.d.). *Wikipedia*. Retrieved December 14, 2015, from https://en.wikipedia.org/wiki/Arnold_Schwarzenegger

Bonigala, M. (n.d.). *The very first UK trademark*. Retrieved from https://www.spellbrand.com/the-very-first-uk-trademark

Breuer, W., & Quinten, B. (2009, July 1). *Cultural finance*. Retrieved from http://ssrn.com/abstract=1282068 https://doi.org/10.2139/ssrn.1282068

Budzich, M. (2011, November 16). *Adam Małysz ponownie w reklamie Teekanne (jest lepiej?)* [Blog post]. Retrieved from http://www.mediafun.pl/adam-malysz-ponownie-w-reklamie-teekanne-jest-lepiej

Cavanagh, C. (2010, June 15). Cristiano Ronaldo poses as the new face of Emporio Armani Underwear and Armani Jeans. *New York Daily News*. Retrieved from http://www.nydailynews.com/entertainment/gossip/cristiano-ronaldo-poses-new-face-emporio-armani-underwear-armani-jeans-article-1.182467

Colapinto, J. (2011, October 3). Famous names. Does it matter what a product is called? *The New Yorker*. Retrieved from http://www.newyorker.com/magazine/2011/10/03/famous-names

Corliss, R. (2012, November 15). *Photos on facebook generate 53% more likes than the average post.* Retrieved from http://blog.hubspot.com/blog/tabid/6307/bid/33800/Photos-on-Facebook-Generate-53-More-Likes-Than-the-Average-Post-NEW-DATA.aspx

Czerwonka, M. (2015). *Charakterystyka wskaźników modelu kulturowego Hofstede.* Retreived from http://kolegia.sgh.waw.pl/pl/KZiF/struktura/IF/konferencje/Documents/M_Czerwonka.pdf

Eminem reklamuje swoje rodzinne miasto. (2009, April 6). *Eminem reklamuje swoje rodzinne miasto.* Retrieved from http://www.hip-hop.pl/news/projector.php?id=1239050906

Eyetracking w e-mail marketingu. Raport, 2013. (2013). Retrieved from http://www.edisonda.pl/mailingi

Fedczyszyn, A. (2014, December 3) *Storytelling, czyli jak stworzyć porywającą historię marki.* Retrieved from http://www.marketing101.pl/story-telling

Fidalgo, P. (2014, September 9). *7 reasons to retire in Portugal by John Malkovich.* Retrieved from http://portugalisparadise.wordpress.com/2014/09/09/7-reasons-to-retire-in-portugal-by-john-malkovich

Fitzpatrick, T. (2012, August 27). Julia Roberts's new Lancôme perfume commercial. *Elle.* Retrieved from http://www.elle.com/beauty/news/a15258/julia-roberts-lancome-perfume-commercial-video-la-vie-est-belle

Foster, C., Punjaisri, K., & Cheng, R. (2010). Exploring the relationship between corporate, internal and employer branding. *Journal of Product & Brand Management, 19*(6), 401–409.

Frączyk, J. (2015, July 22). Coca-Cola podniosła ceny napojów. Zyski spółki wzrosły powyżej najlepszych prognoz. *Money.pl.* Retrieved from http://www.money.pl/gielda/wiadomosci/artykul/coca-cola-podniosla-ceny-napojow-zyski,69,0,1864517.html

Gesteland, R. (2005). *Cross-cultural business behavior: Negotiating, selling, sourcing and managing across cultures.* Copenhagen, Denmark: Copenhagen Business School Press.

Heritage, S. (2012, October 16). Brad Pitt's Chanel No 5 ad: The smell of disaster. *The Guardian.* Retrieved from http://www.theguardian.com/fashion/fashionblog/2012/oct/16/brad-pitt-chanel-no-5-smell-disaster

Hibbert, C. (2008, January 10). Golden celebration for 'oldest brand'. *BBC News.* Retrieved from http://news.bbc.co.uk/2/hi/uk_news/england/london/7180268.stm

Hill, N. (2013). *Myśl i bogać się* [original, *Think and grow rich*, published 1937]. Warsaw, Poland: Wydawnictwo Studio Emka, Warszawa 2013.

Hofstede, G., & Hofstede, J. (1997). *Cultures and organizations. Software of the mind.* New York: McGraw-Hill.

Joanna Krupa: 'I'd rather go naked than wear fur. (n.d.). Retrieved from http://www.peta.org/features/joanna-krupa-anti-fur-ads

Johnson, K. (2015, March 5). Review: 'Ennion,' at the Met, profiles an ancient glassmaker. *The New York Times*. Retrieved from http://www.nytimes.com /2015/03/06/arts/design/review-ennion-at-the-met-profiles-an-ancient-gla ssmaker.html

Kisiel, A. (2015, May 28). *Louis Vuitton i Chanel warte jeszcze więcej! NIKE największą marką odzieżową*. Retrieved from http://vumag.pl/newsy/louis-vui tton-i-chanel-warte-jeszcze-wiecej-nike-najwieksza-marka-odzie-zowa/6z1nmv

Kiszluk, G., & Nowacki, M. (2015, July 10). *Twardoch dumą Mercedesa*. Retrieved from http://www.brief.pl/arty-kul,3052,twardoch_duma_mercedesa.html

Klein, N. (2004). *No logo*. Warsaw, Poland: Świat Literacki.

Kłosiński, J. (n.d.). Kłosiński [Blog]. Retrieved from http://www.klosinski.net

Koniewski, M. (2012). *Świadomość marki a lojalność konsumentów*. Retreived from http://www.research-pmr.com/pl/userfiles/file/wp/swiadomosc-marki-a -lojalnosc-konsumentow.pdf

Kucharski, S. (2013, August 21). Znani polscy aktorzy walczą z homofobią. Nakręcili film o tym, jak obsesja może zniszczyć życie. *Wyborcza*. Retrieved from http://wyborcza.pl/1,76842,14471316,Znani_polscy_aktorzy_walcza _z_homofo-bia__Nakrecili.html

Licencja Gessler – jak ona to robi. (2007, November 22). *Forbes*. Retrieved from http://www.forbes.pl/artykuly/sekcje/sekcja-strategie/licencja-gessler---jak-ona -to---robi,1911,3

Listwan, T. (Ed.). (2005). *Słownik zarządzania kadrami*. Warsaw, Poland: C.H. Beck.

Liu, Z., & Huang, X. (2005). Changes in reading behaviour over the past ten years. *Journal of Documentation, 61*(6), 700–712.

Lontos, P. (2009, December 16). 7 Publicity myths that can hurt your business. *Exchange Morning Post*. Retrieved from http://www.exchangemagazine.com/ morningpost/2009/week51/Wednesday/121611.htm

Majendie, M. (2015, August 21). Usain Bolt: The secret behind the world's fastest man. *CNN*. Retrieved from http://edition.cnn.com/2015/08/21/sport/wo rld-championships-jamaican-sprinting

Makarenko, V. (2010, September 21). Aktor i bank: stare małżeństwo. Historia związku Kondrata z ING. *Wyborcza.biz*. Retrieved from http://wyborcza.pl /1,75248,8398306,Aktor_i_bank__stare_malzenstwo__Historia_zwiazku_ Kondrata.html

Matthew McCanaughey w reklamie samochodu Lincoln MKX. (n.d.). Retrieved from http://www.wirtualnemedia.pl/artykul/matthew-mcconaughey-w-reklamie-samochodu-lincoln-mkx

Maverick, L. A. (1942). The term "maverick" applied to unbranded cattle. *California Folklore Quarterly, 1*, 94–96.

Meggs, P. B. (1998). *A history of graphic design*. Somerset, NJ: Wiley.

Mooney, P., (2008, March 6). *Bite the wax tadpole?* Retrieved from http://www.coca-colacompany.com/stories/2008/03/bite-the-wax-ta

Nurska, K. (2012, July 17). *Świadomości marki, wpływ reklamy na markę* [Blog post]. Retrieved from https://przegladmarketingowy.wordpress.com/2012/07/17/swiadomosci-markiwplyw-reklamy-na-marke

Pawlenka, M. (2014, October 2). Wybory 2014: Z poparciem Piotra Uszoka. Marcin Krupa kandydatem na prezydenta Katowic! TVS. Retrieved from http://www.tvs.pl/informacje/wybory-2014-z-poparciem-piotra-uszoka-marcin-krupa-kandydatem-na-prezydenta-katowic

Peters, T. (2003). *Movers & shakers: The 100 most influential figures in modern business.* London: Basic Books.

Piłkarze jedzą banany! Akcja przeciwko rasizmowi. (2014, April 29). Retrieved from http://sport.se.pl/pilka-nozna/pilka-nozna/pilkarze-jedza-banany-akcja-przeciwko-rasizmowi-zdjecia_395025.html

Polskie gwiazdy mówią 'nie czytaj.' Zabawna kampania Dnia Książki. (2012, April 16). *Dziennik.* Retrieved from http://kultura.dziennik.pl/ksiazki/artykuly/387365,polskie-gwiazdy-w-kampanii-promujacej-czytelnictwo-z-okazji-swiatowego-dnia-ksiazki.html

Rampersad, H. K. (n.d.). *Barack Obama's authentic dream and personal brand.* Retrieved from http://www.myarticlearchive.com/articles/8/267.htm

Ritson, M. (2006, January 11). Mark Ritson on branding: Norse fire smokes out bland brands. *Marketing Magazine.* Retrieved from http://www.marketingmagazine.co.uk/article/534969/mark-ritson-branding-norse-fire-smokes-bland-brands

Rudawska, E. (2008). *Znaczenie relacji z klientami w procesie kształtowania wartości przedsiębiorstwa.* Szczecin, Poland: Wydawnictwa Naukowe Uniwersytetu Szczecińskiego.

Rush, B. C. (2014, August 28). Science of storytelling: Why and how to use it in your marketing. *The Guardian.* Retrieved from http://www.theguardian.com/media-network/media-network-blog/2014/aug/28/science-storytelling-digital-marketing

Schawbel, D. (2010). *Me 2.0. 4 Steps to building your future.* New York: Kaplan Publishing.

Simpson, D. (2012). Modele analizowania różnorodności kulturowej w biznesie międzynarodowym. *Wyzwania gospodarki globalnej. Prace i materiały Instytutu Handlu Zagranicznego Uniwersytetu Gdańskiego, 31,* 602–604.

Smolicki, A. (n.d.). *Gwiazdy i celebryci w reklamach, czyli produkt nie zawsze jest najważniejszy* [Blog post]. Retrieved from http://www.newcreative.pl/blog/e-biznes/gwiazdy-i-celebryci-w-reklamach-czyli-produkt-nie-zawsze-najważniejszy

Snyder, B. (2015, November 3). George Clooney's Nespresso ad. *Fortune.* Retrieved from http://fortune.com/2015/11/03/george-clooneys-nespresso-ad

Sornoso, E. (2015, April 15). Snapchat w marketingu online. *Sprawny Marketing.* Retrieved from http://sprawnymarketing.pl/snapchat-marketing

Statista. (2015). *Number of monthly active facebook users worldwide.* Retrieved from http://www.statista.com/statistics/264810/number-of-monthly-active-facebook-users-worldwide

Storia della Fornaci Georgi. (n.d.). Retrieved from http://www.antichefornaci.it/storia

Szewczyk, P. (2014, May 15). Najpopularniejsza „łyżwa" świata – historia marki Nike. *Biznesflow.* Retrieved from http://biznesflow.pl/historia-marki-nike

Sznajder, A. (2012). *Alianse marketingowe. Partnerstwa przedsiębiorstw dla zwiększenia konkurencyjności.* Warsaw, Poland: Wydawnictwo Oficyna.

Sztompka, P. (2002). *Socjologia.* Warsaw, Poland: Wydawnictwo Znak.

Tata Motors partners with the football legend – Lionel Messi as the global brand ambassador for its passenger vehicles. (2015). [Press release]. Retrieved from http://www.tatamotors.com/press/tata-motors-partners-with-the-football-legend-lionel-messi-as-the-global-brand-ambassador-for-its-passenger-vehicles

The Coca-Cola Company maintains the longest continuous relationship with the Olympic Movement. (n.d.). Retrieved from http://www.olympic.org/sponsors/coca-cola

Thomas, J. (2009, May 14). Kaka stars in Gatorade press campaign. *Marketing Magazine.* Retrieved from http://www.marketingmagazine.co.uk/article/906070/kaka-stars-gatorade-press-campaign

Trusz, F. (2015, October 12). *Jurgen Klopp i Opel Insignia. Stara miłość nie rdzewieje.* Retrieved from http://moto.pl/MotoPL/1,88389,19008875,jurgen-klopp-i-opel-insignia-stara-milosc-nie-rdzewieje.html

Urzędowska, M. (2012, November 6). Aktorzy, raperzy, gwiazda porno: kto z Obamą, kto z Romneyem? I komu to pomoże? *Wyborcza.* Retrieved from http://wyborcza.pl/1,76842,12804614,Aktorzy__raperzy__gwiazda_porno__kto_z_Obama__kto.html

What is storytelling? (n.d.). Retrieved from http://www.storynet.org/resources/whatisstorytelling.html

Wiecej reklam napojow w magazynach i kinach Coca-Cola z dwa razy większym budżetem od Pepsi. (2015, July 13). Retrieved from http://www.wirtualnemedia.pl/artykul/wiecej-reklam-napojow-w-magazynach-i-kinach-coca-cola-z-dwa-razy-wiekszym-budzetem-od-pepsi

Wizerunek w internecie a szukanie pracy. (2011, September 11). Retrieved from http://www.praca.pl/centrum-prasowe/komunikaty-prasowe/wizerunek-w-internecie-a-szukanie-pracy_cp-666.html

CHAPTER 3

Personal Branding and the Challenges of the Information Revolution

Abstract This chapter characterizes the process of shaping a personal brand with an overview of the challenges posed by the information revolution. This chapter includes a comparison of traditional methods of shaping a personal brand and e-branding. It presents the characteristic traits of each strategy and places them into the broader context of generational differences among message recipients. It illustrates the marketing potential of the Internet with examples of effective e-branding campaigns.

Keywords Information revolution • Methods • E-branding • Traditional branding • Branding strategies • Generations

TRADITIONAL WAYS OF SHAPING A PERSONAL BRAND

In the traditional model of personal branding, television played a huge role. Created for it and making its way into social consciousness is the concept of celebrities—people who are generally known, arouse interest and frequently appear in the mass media, especially on television. Celebrities are known not because of their accomplishments, but as an effect of the frequency of their exposure in the media.

The most popular definition of celebrities is that by Daniel Boorstin (1964), according to which a celebrity is "a person who is known for his well-knownness" (p. 57). As Tomasz Olczyk (2013) emphasizes, "the concept draws attention to the tautological nature of the 'celebrity' form

M. Grzesiak, *Personal Brand Creation in the Digital Age*,
https://doi.org/10.1007/978-3-319-69697-3_3

of fame and how it is not supported by any actual accomplishments" (p. 72). Another well-known researcher of the phenomenon, David Marshall (1997), writes that celebrities are people who "in the public sphere, a cluster of individuals are given greater presence and a wider scope of activity and agency than are those who make up the rest of the population. They are followed to move on the public stage while the rest of us watch" (p. ix).

Media presence translates into recognizability, which depends on the frequency of exposure and its reach. "The moment when they [stars] receive heavy media exposure, they often become an easily assimilable symbol, perceived by many like a real friend. Thanks to new media, and especially social media profiles, fans become participants in the life of such stars. They know who they are with, what they are eating, where they go shopping, and what they think about controversial social topics" (Guzek, 2012, p. 120).

An important role is played by closed galas or industry celebrations in the creation of a brand, especially those that are widely covered by the media for a wider public, such as in Poland the annual Journalists' Ball, Sports Champions' Gala, the festive awarding of news magazine awards such as *Polityka* Passports or Person of the Year by the weekly *Wprost*. Every year, many personalities appear at such festivities, strengthening their own brand in those circles, for example journalist Monika Olejnik attends the Journalists' Ball every year, and karate medalist Anna Lewandowska appears at every Sports Champions' Gala.

An image can also be built by combining resources—this is most clearly visible in the case of celebrity couples. The private lives of stars, and especially their intimate relations, are a subject of constant interest in the media. If a celebrity's chosen partner is also a well-known person, their relationship rivets more attention and ensures that media talk about the couple all the more. An example of this kind of media relationship was the relationship of football goalkeeper Radosław Majdan with the singer Doda, and currently his marriage to television presenter Małgorzata Rozenek.

There is a wide range of sites, magazines or programs that specialize in gossip and information about scandals with stars as the main characters. Their content is often based on common knowledge, unconfirmed information, and the subjective opinions of the authors. They create a false, stereotypical image that does not reflect reality. Their activity is mainly dedicated to gaining wide popularity by publishing sensational or scandalous information about the private lives of stars (Gruchoła & Kruczek, 2013, p. 145).

The situation is similar when, in order to build a brand, a scandal is intentionally provoked and publicized, as it was, for example, in the case of Paris Hilton. Until 2004, this heiress of a hotel chain family was essentially unknown. After the ostensibly accidental leak of a sex tape involving her ("10 seks-taśm, którymi", 2014), Paris Hilton was talked about everywhere, and her recognizability rose significantly. It was similar in the case of Kim Kardashian, whose celebrity popularity only began with the release of her sex tape, from which, according to expert calculations, she earned $3 million. ("10 seks-taśm, którymi", 2014).

Another tool that serves to arouse this type of interest from the media is intentional provocation. These include the onstage image (like in the case of Madonna ["Madonna: dziewczyna, która", 2016] or Miley Cyrus ["Kolejna prowokacja Miley Cyrus", 2015]), religious provocations, often bordering on the sacrilegious (Madonna's photo session with a crucifix ["Madonna zabawia się krzyżem", 2010], Polish musician Nergal tearing up a Bible onstage [Podgórska, 2014]), or expressing controversial views publicly (racist comments by Kuba Wojewódzki and Michał Figurski on the radio ["Wojewódzki i Figurski ponownie", 2012]).

Many stars base their image on a foundation of consistency—they show the image they created for a particular industry in the media in every situation, including offstage (an example might be the behavior of Lady Gaga or Doda). There is a consistency between how they appear onstage and the answers they give in interviews, the choice of social events they appear at, publicized parts of their private lives and so on. A similar goal is served by consistently accepting similar roles in the case of film and television actors, in order to strengthen the perception of their personal brand in a certain way (an example might be Katarzyna Figura, who always plays in roles in which she is a sex symbol, or Bogusław Linda, who always chooses roles of a hard, uncommonly masculine hero).

Increasing the recognizability of one's own brand is also served by introducing signature products. This often also helps to create positive associations with the person owing to a luxury product or perfume. Today, many stars have their own line of perfume (for example, Paris Hilton, Jennifer Lopez, Celine Dion or Mariah Carey), but this fashion was started by Elizabeth Taylor at the end of the 1980s. Endorsed with Taylor's name, the perfumes Passion and White Diamonds earned Elizabeth Arden over $1 billion in profit. In a *Forbes* ranking, these are the best-selling perfumes in history (Goldman, 2012). Not only do perfumes play such a role: actress Scarlett Johansson lends her name to an entire line of cosmetics,

Britney Spears a line of intimate wear, and on the Polish market, an example might be Marek Kondrat and his chain of select wine shops bearing his name, *Kondrat Wina Wybrane.*

A personal brand can also be built through association with other recognized brands, such as through appearing in advertisements or accepting the role of brand ambassador. Over 20% of all television ads in the United States involve a personality, and around 10% of all television advertising expenses are fees for these personalities. Some researchers suggest that the use of personalities increases the marginal value of advertising expenditures and creates brand capital through repeated association of the personality with the brand (Awdziej & Tkaczyk, 2002). We can observe a similar trend in Poland. For years, Szymon Majewski has been the face of the largest Polish bank (PKO BP); Juliette Binoche makes ads for Crédit Agricole; actor Piotr Fronczewski for Getin Bank; and Olympic champion Justyna Kowalczyk appears in advertising spots for Polbank. Hubert Urbański, known as the host of many television shows, was the face of Bank Millennium. One of the most talked-about marriages between a bank and a personality is between ING Bank Śląski and Marek Kondrat. Why did ING decide specifically on this figure? Because Kondrat, who is not only a popular actor known for his many film and theater roles, but also as an entrepreneur operating his own chain of stores offering rare wines, is thought of as a well-off, wealthy person and, what is more, one not embroiled in any controversies (Dołhasz, 2009, p. 73).

Aside from the indubitable benefits in terms of image (for both sides), appearing in an advertising campaign is highly profitable for stars. Television advertisements featuring Marek Kondrat cost over PLN 67 million (ca. $16.5 million). For advertisements featuring Hubert Urbański, Bank Millennium spent PLN 49.3 million (ca. $12.3 million), and the participation of international stars like Antonio Banderas, John Cleese, Danny DeVito or Gérard Depardieu is associated with advertising production costs of around PLN 40 million (ca. $10 million) (Godzic, 2012, pp. 43–44).

Similar benefits come from accepting the role of a brand ambassador, provided that the given brand represents the values that the star identifies with, reflects his or her lifestyle, or allows building the kind of image that the star aspires to. An example of this is the cooperation between Mercedes-Benz and Szczepan Twardoch ("Nie składałem ślubów ubóstwa", 2015), Opel and Łukasz Jakóbiak ("Opel rozpoczyna jedyną", 2015), or among global stars, Tiger Woods and TAG Heuer (Sinha, 2012), or Julia Roberts and Calzedonia ("Calzedonia chooses Julia Roberts", 2015).

It is not only the support of commercial brands that can have a positive influence on a person's image, but supporting the activities of non-governmental organizations or of some cause or group of people may do so as well. One of the most highly recognized activities of this kind is being a UNICEF Goodwill Ambassador (a role currently filled by Katy Perry, Liam Neeson and Serena Williams, among others [UNICEF, n.d.]), or a UNHCR Goodwill Ambassador (including writer Khaled Hosseini, whereas Angelina Jolie plays the role of special envoy for refugees). Many personalities join in forms of activism, such as Joanna Krupa fighting for animal rights and opposing the wearing of natural fur ("Joanna Krupa przeciwko hodowli", 2015), or establish their own foundations and associations (for example, the Leonardo DiCaprio Foundation engages in the fight against global warming, leonardodicaprio.org).

An important role in building one's image is played by positioning oneself as an expert and a person who has achieved financial success—this also draws media interest and secondarily leads to an increase in popularity. This is how it works in the case of experts (jurors) or singer Kora on *Must Be the Music*), but also specialists taking part in television shows organized for them, for example, chefs competing with each other on *Top Chef*. Holding media interest is also served by participation in other competitive spectacles—well-known people compete with each other on various programs like *Dancing with the Stars, Celebrity Splash!*, or the Polish production *Gwiazdy Tańczą na Lodzie* [*Stars Dancing on Ice*].

In order remain in the media, many celebrities decide to publish their own book. Just like talent shows, books not only help maintain popularity, but also display it. The phenomenon of celebrity books appeared on the Polish book market at the beginning of 2010 with the release of books by stars such as actress Kasia Cichopek, television host Krzysztof Ibisz, presenter and journalist Kinga Rusin and producer Weronika Marczuk. These were high print-run editions that reached high positions on the bestseller lists. Each was widely discussed in the media, but the interest in them was relatively short, because readers and the media are continuously waiting for new celebrity book proposals (Kasperek, 2014, p. 74).

Of secondary importance is whether stars choose to write a book themselves or to use the services of a ghostwriter, whether they give interviews in book form or hire an author to write their authorized biography. These publications have much in common—the cover is made in the same way (always with the star's picture), the books contain a range of color illustrations and the text itself is set into columns with large fonts (usually like a tabloid). The promotional campaign is conducted in a similar way: interviews with the authors, book signings and meetings, and reviews on gossip websites (Kasperek, 2014, p. 75).

Sale of these books is possible thanks to the previously created brand, and at the same time the very appearance of a publication with this brand reinforces, strengthens and broadens its popularity. Publishing a book has also become a splendid pretext for the presence of the author in the media, which in many cases opens the door for a former star to return to peak popularity (Kasperek, 2014, p. 81).

A well-established brand helps when taking up work in a new field, promotion is then built on the basis of name recognition. An example of this might be Michael Jordan opening his own restaurant, Michael Jordan's Steak House (mjshchicago.com), or Nergal opening a men's barbershop— Barberian Academy & Barber Shop (Sosin, 2014).

THE MARKETING POTENTIAL OF THE INTERNET

The Development of Digital Marketing

Over the past dozen or so years, we can observe a strengthening of the area of digital marketing, which is capturing more and more of the advertising market. Digital marketing has undergone several phases of development. In the first phase, thanks to the development of email, there was improved contact with the base of clients and consumers. The second phase brought the popularity of web pages at the cost of product catalogs or advertising brochures. In the third phase, online stores appeared, price comparison websites, and consumer service sites. In the fourth phase, the digital marketing scene was complimented by social media offering entirely new ways both of reaching customers, as well as conducting advertising campaigns or sales. In the fifth phase, the market for digital marketing was supplemented by videoblogs, transmission of information by video in real time via live streaming, as well as mobile marketing (Dziekoński, 2014, pp. 13–14).

The classical concept of a marketing mix, developed in the 1960s by Jerome McCarthy, describes five elements (product, price, distribution, promotion and personnel, in other words, 5P), through which we can influence the market. It has taken on a new dimension in the era of digital marketing. Dziekoński (2014) describes the value added by new media as follows:

(a) Product—individualized offers; products created for individual orders can have national reach instead of only regional, as had been the case previously.
(b) Price—a significant increase in the negotiating power of customers thanks to online auctions, group purchasing and price comparison sites.
(c) Distribution—the inexpensive and widely accessible distribution channel of e-commerce is changing the rules of traditional trade in many industries.
(d) Promotion—two-way communication instead of one-way, end of the era of classical advertising, communication based on interaction, communication simultaneously among consumers.
(e) Personnel (service)—competition not only in quality of service, but also with customer time savings, for example, waiting time for an email response (p. 21).

Expenditures for Online Advertising

Although the most money from advertising still goes to television, the greatest increase in advertising expenditures is seen in iInternet advertising. For example, while in the first quarter of 2012 advertising expenditures rose 3.1% overall, in Internet advertising there was an increase on the order of 12.1%. The greatest increase was seen in the Middle East and Africa (35.2%), in Latin America (31.8%), and in Europe (12.1%) (Dziekoński, 2014).

In 2013, the share of television in global advertising expenditures was 39.6%, in second place was Internet advertising (18.3%), next newspapers (16.8%), magazines (8%), outdoor and radio (6.9% each), mobile advertising (2.9%), and cinema (0.6%).

In 2016, the share of television in global advertising expenditures dropped to 38.3%. In the same year the share of newspapers fell to 13.2%, magazines to 6.4%, outdoor advertising to 6.8% and radio to 6.4%. The share of cinema advertising remained unchanged (0.6%). In 2016, the share of global advertising expenditures that went to Internet advertising rose to 19.7%, and mobile advertising to 8.6%.

At present, expenditures on advertising for mobile devices—smartphones and tablets—show growth six-times faster than for desktop systems. According to a forecast by ZenithOptimedia, the rise in mobile advertising expenditures will continue at 51%, while the growth in expenditures for desktop devices was predicted at only 8%. ("Polski rynek reklamy będzie rósł", 2014).

According to estimates by ZenithOptimedia, advertisers in 2016 dedicated 23.6% of the total advertising budgets to Internet advertising. This means that the expenditures for online advertising for the first time exceeded those for advertising in newspapers and magazines combined (22.7%). The difference between the shares of the Internet and the largest medium, television, also shrank, from 15.9% to 9.9% ("Polski rynek reklamy będzie rósł", 2014).

The Development of E-commerce

E-commerce is developing just as dynamically. As shown in the report *E-commerce w Polsce 2015* (2015), online buyers have ever-greater awareness of e-commerce brands and services that are available on the Internet. When shopping online, they most of all look for convenience, savings and the greater selection compared to traditional stores. Aside from making purchases, users declared that they search for and compare prices, using mainly the pages of online stores and search engines. The main motivation for online shoppers, other than low prices, is the convenience associated with 24/7 access, the lack of any need to be physically present in the store and the ease of comparing prices offered on the marketplace ("E-commerce w Polsce", 2015, p. 8).

The results of empirical research unambiguously show that in Poland the interest in e-shopping is constantly growing.[1] Among all Internet users, 17 million (78%) visit e-commerce sites, and 21.7 million (59%) e-stores. From 2010 to 2015, the growth in the number of Internet users interested in the topic of e-commerce rose 36 % (from 13.08 million to 17.73 million). In the same period, the number of Internet users rose by 30% (Raport na temat wartości polskiego rynku, n.d.). Customer interest in online services also grew, with a resulting increase in the number of electronic payments. The estimated value of the Polish e-commerce market in 2015 is PLN 33 billion (ca. $8.25 billion).

Growth in the Number of Internet Users

Over the course of only 12 years, the number of regular Internet users increased from 350 million in 2000 to ca. 2 billion in 2012. According to a report by comScore, the greatest increase in the number of internet users, as much as 62% compared to 2011, was noted in Venezuela. The next places are held by India (34%) and Indonesia (29%). The highest number of Internet users are residents of Asia. In 2011, they made up nearly 45%. Europe in this ranking takes second place (22%), and placing third is North America (12%). It is estimated that ca. 33% of residents have access to the Internet. For example, this ratio is currently 80% for the United States, and for Europe, 61%. Poland is above the European average at ca. 62% (Surmacz, 2014, p. 33). In addition, 62% of Polish Internet users declared in 2014 that they had an account with least one social media service, and this number is growing each year (CBOS, 2014, p. 14).

Taking into consideration only the period from March 2007 to November 2011, the number of people using the Internet in the world grew by 88%, and the number using social media by as much as 174% (Roszkowski, 2013, p. 337). Research published by Nielsen in December 2012 shows that the average amount of time using social media is also steadily growing—in the United States it grew by 37% (Roszkowski, 2013, p. 337).

Smartphonization

As research published in the report *Polska jest mobi 2015* (as cited in Szylar, 2015, p. 174) showed, mobile devices dominated the Polish market for devices with Internet access. The number of people who have a laptop is constantly growing—in 2015 82.71% of Internet users declared that they owned one. Nearly as many declared that they owned a smartphone (74.8%) or a mini tablet (63%). A drop in the number of people who own a desktop computer was also noted—in 2015 this was reported as 62.24% of users (Szylar, 2015, pp. 173–174).

Advantages of Social Media

Social media have become a form of social broadcast medium, with content created by consumers themselves and not institutions. Free and widespread evaluation of commenting on social media, as well as the creation of content and distribution of information has earned social media greater credibility than content distributed via the press or television (Kaznowski, 2014, pp. 74–75).

Institutional media, even those that remain in private hands, are subject to various kinds of restrictions, even pressure from governments—through licenses or concessions—whereas social media is solely under the control of society itself. They are characterized by much greater openness, an orientation toward dialog, opinions and the exchange of views, which accounts for their growing popularity. In traditional media, only professionals can create content, whereas in social media everyone has free access not only to receiving content, but above all to creating it. An undoubted advantage of social media is that the delay time between creation and publication is kept to a minimum.

E-branding and Traditional Branding

The television, press and radio of decades past allowed access to mass consumers and delivered controlled messages to them. In one-way marketing communication, still widely used in the 1990s, a brand built its image and its value through messages delivered to consumers by way of the press, television, radio or forms of outdoor advertising: posters, billboards and flyers. Today, however, in a world dominated by new technologies, the efficacy of traditional messages is falling.

As an analysis conducted by the McKinsey consulting firm, the current efficacy of television advertising in the United States is at only one third of the level of the number of viewers that it reached only 20 years ago (Kall, 2015, p. 11). The Ehrenberg-Bass Institute for Marketing Science conducted a study that showed that only one sixth of all advertisements on television were remembered and correctly associated with the brand six days after broadcast. (as cited in Kall, 2015, p. 11). The number of viewers of the big television networks is also constantly falling,[2] as is the average amount of time spent in front of the television, especially among the youngest age group of television viewers (Połowianiuk, 2015).

Viewers expect interaction, and so aside from traditional branding, e-branding is appearing more and more frequently. Effective brand communication demands presence online—as research has shown, the growth of income of those who use social media to communicate with customers is 25% faster than for those who do not use them (Kall, 2015, p. 167).

Online brand communication permits interactivity, creates the ability to obtain feedback on reactions to the message, receive opinions about products, activities and services. The Internet facilitates communication along the brand–consumer line, making immediate sharing of information and reactions to newly appearing circumstances possible. Currently, a potential customer works out an opinion about a brand, assesses its credibility and whether to trust it mainly on the basis of its image on the Internet.

Traditional Branding

As Elliot and Percy show, a brand in fact only exists in the mind of a consumer, and so management of a brand is management of perception. A brand is an entire product on offer (and not just the name, trademark and so on) which is meant to guarantee the purchaser something exceptional—in terms of use or symbolically—and at the same time influence the decision process, offering more than a "generic" product, that is, one without any particular brand (as cited in Kall, 2015, p. 16).

The goals of both traditional branding as well as e-branding are:

(a) to provide information about the brand—the direct goal of image messages directed at consumers is not sales, but to make the brand itself sellable by delivering information about its usefulness
(b) to build brand awareness—because people generally prefer that which they know, the first step to building a brand image is to build awareness of it among consumers
(c) to engage consumers in a relationship with the brand—the goal of branding is to create affinities along the brand–consumer line, which make the brand more attractive in the eyes of customers, more desirable and worthy of recommendation, so that customers, because the brand meets their expectations, become loyal to it (Kall, 2015, p. 28).

Characteristics of Traditional Branding

The main characteristic of traditional branding is a monodirectional channel of communication from the sender to the client. This narrow elite of senders determined the content of the message. This is also linked to the monopoly on communication of the traditional media. In this message, there is essentially no place for any content created by receivers, not counting those who pass through a verification phase by the sender (for example, letters to the editor). This has to do with the high costs of access to marketing tools, which results in these being in the hands of a limited group of senders (Królewski & Sala, 2014, p. 13).

Channels of Communication

Traditional branding uses defined channels of communication: television, radio, the press and outdoor advertising. As in the traditional ways of brand creation, one should also include sponsorship activities as well as organizing events.

The traditional media have been used successfully for years in the process of creating brand images. Seen globally, today the most frequently used marketing medium is television, which has a 40% share of the market, followed by advertising the in the press (newspapers and magazines), to which 25% of global advertising expenditures are directed (Kall, 2015, p. 194). Although in the past decade a substantial flow of resources toward new media can be seen, traditional marketing received almost 78% of expenditures on advertising campaigns (Kall, 2015, p. 15). Advertisers reach for traditional channels especially in campaigns directed toward older generations.

Personal Recommendations

Personal recommendations are the most effective type of marketing available, especially recommendations by friends and acquaintances. Research has shown that as much as 90% of people trust the recommendations of others (Kall, 2015, p. 17). One of the range of traditional tools is word-of-mouth marketing. Its role is to reach consumers with a direct message that takes the form of a "spontaneous" recommendation. The goal of this strategy for brand creation is usually to create a buzz surrounding the product, service or person being promoted (Thomas, 2004, pp. 64–72). An example of this kind of activity in its traditional form might be sending out free samples to volunteer agents (who are to share their impressions with their friends), or finding celebrity brand ambassadors, who support the product with their own image. However, the most effective form of recommendation marketing remains recommendation by friends.

Out-of-Home Advertising
Creating an image via the OOH (out-of-home) advertising channel is one of the dominant tools of traditional branding. In Poland, expenditures on outdoor campaigns have remained fairly level for a number of years—PLN 450 million (approximately $110 million) in 2013 and 2014 ("Raport IGRZ o wynikach reklamy OOH", 2015). This type of advertising is associated with the ability to reach social groups preferred by the advertiser, especially urban residents, where outdoor advertising is used widely. Tools such as OOH can be flexibly adapted to groups of receivers taking into consideration geographic considerations (a particular city, region or country but also, for example, all private colleges and universities in a country). The message flowing from outdoor advertising focuses on pictures, through which an advertiser can precisely define the image of the product advertised. A unique trait of outdoor advertising is how the receiver cannot avoid contact with its content, and so involuntarily registers the message transmitted. Despite its traditional form, outdoor advertising may still be used in innovative branding campaigns. An example of this is the 2013 IBM campaign which used items of their own industrial design (for example, rain shelters for pedestrians, benches) to place their brand logo on. These actions helped to associate the IBM brand with innovation and user-friendliness (Kiefaber, 2013).

The Internet as the Dominant Communication Channel
Technological development has meant that an increasing number of potential recipients, for messages designed to create a brand image, are made up of Internet users. The internet is the dominant channel of communication, particularly among the youngest generations. Currently in the European Union, over 70% of all individuals use the Internet, of whom 47% do so using smartphones and tablets, having constant access to the net at their fingertips (Trzeciak, 2015, p. 23). The situation is similar in Poland: among Poles, 63% use the Internet (CBOS, 2014), and 71.9% of households have net access. Nearly two in five Poles (39%) also have an account on social media (CBOS, 2014).

Research by Mindshare Polska shows that Poles spend daily:

(a) 3–4 hours in front of a laptop screen
(b) 3 hours at a desktop computer
(c) 2.6 hours with a smartphone
(d) 2 hours in front of the television
(e) 1.6 hours with a tablet (c.f. Kall, 2015, p. 75).

Table 3.1   Percentage division of time consuming media in selected countries

	Cell phone (not counting calls and texts)	Television	Internet (laptop, PC)	Radio	Tablet	Press
World (total)	27	22	19	12	10	9
China	30	17	29	5	12	7
Germany	29	22	20	16	6	7
South Korea	25	23	24	8	11	9
France	19	22	22	13	15	8

Source: J. Kall, *Branding na smartfonie. Komunikacja mobilna marki*, Wolters Kluwer SA, Warsaw, 2015

One can see in these data a great difference in time accessing television messages (2 hours) and online messages (in total for all devices with Internet access—12.2 hours daily).

In highly developed countries—the United States and Great Britain—over the past five years there was as much a sevenfold increase in the amount of time spent using mobile devices (Kall, 2015, p. 77). The percentage division of time consuming media across the world shows that devices with Internet access have a significant preponderance over traditional media (television, radio, press), which is illustrated in Table 3.1.

As a result of this trend, consumer decisions are also increasingly made on the basis of information available on the Internet—users check goods and services on Internet forums and rely on the recommendations of their friends and the opinions available on the communication channels of a given brand on social media.

E-branding and Its Characteristics

E-branding, much like traditional branding, is supposed to create a certain image, but to create and manage a brand it uses the tools and possibilities that the Internet offers.

Although e-branding has the same goals as traditional branding, they differ in several ways. E-branding, as opposed to traditional branding, is characterized by:

(a) Constant presence—traditional forms of marketing communication, for example, advertising on television, in the press or by flyers, constitute a momentary transmission. Communication on the

Internet is constant, all content is always available on Internet pages or social media profiles. E-branding can reach every Internet user anywhere in the world. The cost of online presence, as opposed to traditional forms of branding, are relatively low, especially if their endurance is considered.

(b) Interactivity—communication via the Internet makes it possible to depart from one-way transmission (radio advertising or appearing on television) in favor of interaction with the receiver (Trzeciak, 2015, p. 25). Social media users can follow the channels of particular brands, are kept up-to-date about current actions taken by their preferred brands, have the ability to ask questions, rate or share feedback about products and services, thanks to which companies or individuals are able to react more quickly to user evaluations or to adapt their branding activities and strategies to the needs and expectations of consumers.

(c) Speed—an image campaign in traditional media (television, press, outdoor advertising) requires planning far in advance. Public and media relations also require time. Building lasting relationships with journalists takes months. On the Internet, immediate action is possible, and every piece of information sent via the net (blog entries, newsletters, posts on a social media channel) reaches receivers immediately. What is more, attractive messages spread themselves, thanks to the ability to copy and share their content,[3]

(d) A constantly growing group of receivers—we can currently observe the gradual decline in the number of receivers of traditional media, for example, television or press. At the same time, the number of Internet users is constantly growing,

(e) Building trust—in the case of traditional communication, the reach of the recommendation of a satisfied or an unsatisfied customer was limited. Now, the number of people reached by consumers expressing their opinions is significantly greater, and so every recommendation or negative comment can have a huge influence on the perception of the brand or creation of its image. The Internet, and particularly social media, allow consumers to organize themselves into strong pressure groups that can support a brand, but can also harm it. This is why it is so important in e-branding to care for loyal customers and to gain brand ambassadors who, in a crisis situation, can spontaneously help and support the brand.

Selected Communication Channels and Tools Used in E-branding

Social Media

Channels in social media are currently widely used in brand communication. Their advantage lies in the possible interaction between users and the brand, but also in the creation of relationships between those who follow the brand. Research by DEI Worldwide and OTX have shown that as many as 70% of consumers use social media to find information regarding companies and the products and services they offer, and 20% of them make purchasing decisions based on the information they find. Research by Syncapse has shown that customers who follow a given brand on Facebook are more loyal and spend more on purchases that other customers ("Online branding – potrzeba nowych strategii", n.d.).

Following favorite brands on social media is becoming increasingly popular. Four out of five members of Generation Y using social media sites add the pages of brands to their favorites, among Generation X 31% do, and among the postwar or Baby Boom Generation, 27% do. Users want to stay up to date and know what is currently happening with the given brand. Members of Generation Y, instead of advertising, expect brands to create interesting services and offer access to sponsored content (van den Bergh & Behrer, 2012, p. 38).

Content Marketing

Content marketing is taking on an increasing importance in branding. Creation and distribution of high-quality information is one of the most effective marketing strategies for creating a brand image. Presentation of specialized and free content supports the perception of a brand as trustworthy and professional.

Web Pages

A web page is the most important online calling card of a brand. Its high visibility and easy access increases the credibility of a company and customers' inclination to use its services or products ("Online branding – potrzeba nowych strategii", n.d.). The ordering of Google search results places web pages higher than social media profiles, and so having a brand web page is quite important. Additional positioning mechanisms promote a page (for example, in searching for the word "coaching", pages that contain not only the isolated word "coaching" but also extended content are placed higher), as well as user-friendly services, that is, pages that are readable, clear and have a mobile version.

Buzz Marketing

The terms "buzz marketing", "viral marketing", "word-of-mouth marketing", "evangelist marketing" and many others are used interchangeably (Mazurkiewicz, 2014, p. 38). Today, a significant part of the communication of recommendations takes place online, which is why brands follow the opinions appearing on social media pages so closely. Research has shown that 43% of those aged 15–24 recommend that friends try a brand. Buzz marketing has a great influence on consumer decisions in Generation Y—in as many as 60% of cases, one person can convince another to try a product for the first time (van den Bergh & Behrer, 2012, p. 53).

BRANDING AND E-BRANDING IN THE CONTEXT OF CHOICES BY DIFFERENT GENERATIONS

The Silent Generation

This cohort is variously called the Silent Generation, the Depression Generation, the Swing Generation or traditionalists. These are people born between 1928 and 1945, the children of World War II and of the Great Depression. The moniker "silent" refers to their conformism, and indicates the clear difference between them and the next generations that clearly express their views (van den Bergh & Behrer, 2012, p. 22). They value savings and ethics in business, and important values are social security and family ties. They rely on tried, trusted products and services. Their preferred channels of communication are radio, television, billboards, magazines, traditional mail and meetings with experts (Williams & Page, 2011, p. 3).

This generation is often called the Silent Generation, which according to *Forbes* magazine manifests itself in their tendency not to "flaunt" and a distaste for self-presentation. Born into this generation were most famous world leaders, such as Martin Luther King, Robert F. Kennedy, Che Guevara or Margaret Thatcher. This generation—particularly in highly-developed European countries—became synonymous with millionaires. Many members of this generation made huge fortunes, which was also met with criticism from many, who pointed to their tendency toward enriching themselves to excess. According to a 1993 article in *Time* magazine regarding the religious practices of the Silent Generation, 42% of those surveyed declared that they practic religion regularly and had a specific religious affiliation, while 33% stated that they practiced only occasionally, and yet declared themselves to be deeply religious. In Poland, the Postwar Boom Generation grew up under the realities of socialism, which had a great influence on their attitudes to life. In this generation, there is a strong need for stability. The effect of this is that this generation is characterized, even today, by a resistance to change and a relatively strong mistrust of new technologies. This also explains why this generation sees holding the same lifelong position at the same employer as a sign of safety and a peaceful life.

Postwar Boom Generation

This name applies to those born between 1946 and 1964, after the end of World War II. Other names include the Love Generation, the Woodstock Generation, Baby Boomers, and the Sandwich Generation. People in this cohort enjoyed more freedom, thanks to which they are more flexible and adapt easily (McCrindle & Hooper, 2007). They are characterized by their need for self-sufficiency. It was members of this generation that created the first personal computers and mobile devices. They value individuality, freedom of expression and living by their own rules. Their life goals are prosperity, good health and happiness. They have less trust of authority. Television is their main and preferred medium, but they also use the Internet, although mainly for social development, and only to a small degree as a tool supporting the decision process and choice of brands (Williams & Page, 2011, p. 6).

Generation X

Generation X is made up of people born between 1965 and 1979, who are also called Baby Busters, the New Lost Generation, the Invisible Generation, and the "Why Me?" Generation. This generation fills the gap between two demographic booms: that of the 1950s and that of the end of the twentieth century, which is called the "millennium" boom. Many researchers believe that the demographic decline in the 1960s was the result of the introduction of birth control pills (in 1960), which resulted in a drop in the birth rate. According to two leading demographers, Howe and Strauss (1993), Generation X are the children born in times when society's attention was focused on adults, and not on children. It should also be noted that this generation grew up in times of a rising number of divorces, which began in 1960 and continued to rise until 1980. Moreover, it was also the time of the sexual revolution, not only in the United States, but also in Europe. It has been observed that the childhood of Generation X often lacked adult supervision in the time between the end of the school day and when parents came home from work. Generation X is seen as the first generation raised on MTV: the world presented in the first music videos, and its values system and esthetic tastes were shaped, to a large degree, by music genres like alternative rock, grunge and the first works of hip-hop. The American Social Survey shows that members of this generation were more pessimistic at age 18–29 than those in previous generations were. Such attitudes were prevalent until 1997, when *Time* magazine published the article "Generation X Reconsidered", the main point of which was a revision of the hypothesis of the excessive pessimism of Generation X. The authors also concluded that this generation included the most entrepreneurial individuals, who prefer "to take matters into their own hands." In Poland as well, members of Generation X began their professional careers in the beginning of the 1990s, in a time of recession, mass firings and economic transformation. They are characterized by a high level of individualism and a desire for independence (Mróz, 2013). They are interested in earning money by the method of "buy low, sell high." To a significantly greater degree than other generations, they tend to believe in truth in advertising, and perceive television advertising as attractive (van den Bergh & Behrer, 2012, p. 22). Television is the preferred channel of communication for this generation, but they do use the Internet to educate themselves and to gather information regarding products. In 2011, a research study "Study of Youth" was conducted with financing by the University of Michigan, in which it was determined that Generation X is characterized by the greatest level of happiness compared with other generations. The average level of happiness of members of this generation was 7.5 on a ten-point scale, and as many as 29% of those studied declared their level of happiness to be over 9.

Generation Y

This generation includes people born between 1980 and 1996, is the first generation to grow up in the new millennium and is also called the Millennium Generation, the Why Generation or Net Generation. In contrast to Generation X, Generation Y was raised in a society that turned its attention away from adults and back to children. In this generation, many parents tried to participate in their children's decision making, which unfortunately resulted in a relatively low level of autonomy among members of this generation as adults. The generation is also characterized by a strong sense of self-esteem—these are individuals who were raised in a spirit that any goal can be achieved, and every child is equipped with extraordinary talent in many areas which, in turn, often resulted in a sense of entitlement and great expectations. Members of Generation Y are generally highly ambitious and strongly motivated, but a sense of entitlement is not alien to them.

This generation in Poland grew up in the period of systemic change. It is also the first generation that did not experience the previous system—they know it only from their parents' stories, but they are not able to understand many aspects of it. They are much closer to digital technology, as they could follow its constant development and so were able to master its tools more rapidly and more completely. This generation finds information and entertainment exclusively on the internet and at the same time is the first generation inclined to give up on use of traditional media such as newspapers, radio broadcasts or television stations.

These people have a great amount of knowledge about marketing activities; advertising and media have been with them since birth, and so they are relatively resistant to advertising. New technologies are hugely important to them (van den Bergh & Behrer, 2012, p. 22). Some of the characteristics of members of Generation Y are: ecological awareness, distrust of the media, intensive use of electronic media, awareness of global trends and use of the Internet in the process of making purchasing decisions (Paul, 2001, pp. 42–49). Generation Y, based on research conducted mainly in the United States, is currently seen as the largest market segment in the world today, and its spending it continually growing (Gołąb-Andrzejak, 2014, p. 13). At the same time, the results show that Generation Y does not tolerate poor experiences with brands, and all negative situations can immediately lead to a loss of trust and loyalty. For Generation Y, brand authenticity and integrity are very important—it is only these which potentially can lead to formation of long-term attachment of consumers to a brand (Parris, 2010).

Members of Generation Y use television selectively, concentrating solely on programs made for them. A new, selected channel of distribution in the case of this generation is computer games and product placement within them (Williams & Page, 2011, p. 9).

Generation Z

This generation, which includes all those born after 1996, is also called the iGeneration not only on account of their attachment to their iPods, iPhones and iPads, but also because of their great need for individualization. It is often called the Mobile Generation, because from preschool age onward they have been in contact with devices with Internet access. They are regarded as the foster children of the world of computer games, preferring to read an e-book over a book in traditional form. Personalization of messages is the basis for the thinking of this generation (van den Bergh & Behrer, 2012, p. 24). It is seen as the most able to multi-task of any observed generation. Its members feel well in any life tasks in which conducting many activities simultaneously is required. They are known for being able to talk with someone while simultaneously checking e-mail, text messages and posts on social media. At the same time, it is the generation that has the greatest difficulty concentrating for a longer period—listening to a lecture or presentation longer than two or three minutes is highly uncomfortable for them. They prefer short messages when it comes to online content as well. Many YouTubers, thinking of these viewers, shorten their video materials to two or three minutes. What is more, a message directed toward members of Generation Z should be constructed in such a way as to have a maximal amount of infographic material and a minimal amount of continuous text.

This generation also presents a challenge for many employers, as they do not become attached to a particular job and leave as soon as they realize that the given position does not meet their expectations. They prefer virtual space over real space. It is in this virtual world that they create social relationships, make friends and most of their contacts, mainly people who share their interests. Daniel Goleman points out that this is a generation with the lowest level of emotional intelligence. As a result of their main activity being exploration of the virtual world, they have not acquired the ability to recognize emotions in the facial micro-expressions of others.

Often in real contact with another person in the real world they feel ill at ease and are not able to assess the emotional state of the other person. They learned to evaluate emotions on the basis of the graphic iconography used in Internet messages, and what proceeds from that, without such iconography they feel lost and unable to build proper emotional relationships with another person in the real world.

Among the strong points of Generation Z, one can enumerate their ease of communication with peers from around the world: they are adept in languages (especially in English, which is present in their lives from an early age in the virtual world of computer games and programming) as well as the lack of barriers to "remote" work via the Internet. They are also characterized by a need for great transparency, which does not make them the best to trust with confidential information.

TRADITIONAL BRANDING, E-BRANDING AND BRAND AWARENESS

American research has shown that advertising on the Internet increases spontaneous brand recognition by 4%, and research conducted by the European Interactive Advertising Association in Germany for MSN has revealed that businesses that advertise on the Internet increase their reach by an additional 16%. ("Online branding – potrzeba nowych strategii", n.d.). The results of the research *The Branding Value of Search's Page One* from 2012 show that the most significant growth in building brand awareness—as much as 30%—occurs when a brand appears simultaneously in organic search engine results and in the sponsored results on the first screen ("Online branding—potrzeba nowych strategii", n.d.).

SELECTED EXAMPLES OF THE EFFICACY OF E-BRANDING

McDonald's

As an example of the greater efficacy of e-branding compared to traditional branding, a sandwich campaign conducted by McDonald's in Great Britain may serve well. Transferring 20% of the offline advertising budget to the Internet resulted in a 13% growth in product awareness. If that 20% had been spent on traditional media, the growth in product awareness would have been a mere 2% ("Online branding – potrzeba nowych strategii", n.d.).

Pepsi

A similar route was taken by Pepsi. In 2010, it gave up traditional advertising during the Super Bowl, and $20 million was devoted to a social campaign called the Pepsi Refresh Project. As part of the project, an online platform was created that made it possible to promote local initiatives in need of financing. Every user of the platform could open an account on the service and upload a video regarding their initiative and then receive the votes of other users.

Winning projects received funding from $5000 to $25,000. Because users voted for the projects they found the most interesting, Pepsi could learn about the needs and preferences of its customers. Also taking part in the Pepsi Refresh Project was a well-known American actress Eva Longoria, a star of the series *Desperate Housewives*, who supported the project of the non-profit Padres Contra El Cáncer (van den Bergh & Behrer, 2012, pp. 45–46). The Pepsi project fit ideally to the expectations of Generation Y, and was a good alternative to traditional advertising, which this generation mistrusts, and it engaged users, meeting the criterion of interactivity.

The HBO Series True Blood

The premiere of the third season of the HBO production *True Blood*, in contrast to previous seasons, was promoted online. The campaign was targeted at users of the Flixster and Variety services on mobile devices. Touching the screen while watching the page caused bloody fingerprints to appear, and touching it again made them drip to the bottom of the screen. Next, a banner appeared encouraging viewers to watch the trailer for the next season of the series. Viewership for the third season of *True Blood* rose by 38% compared to the previous one (Kall, 2015, p. 129) This may have to do with the fact that the advertisement met the criterion of interactivity, and by using the mobile channel, it reached members of Generation Y, who watch television much less frequently.

Nike

In 2004 the athletic clothing producer Nike developed an application for runners, Nike+ which, after installation on a smartphone, allowed users to save information about every workout and to publish it on the nikeplus.com service. The technology was synchronized with iPods and iPhones. On the nikeplus.com service, users could take advantage of training regimens, compare their achievements and compete with others. Because of Nike+ the company's sales increased from a 48% share of the athletic shoe market to 61% over the course of two years.

Thanks to the service, many users grew convinced of the brand and its products (Kall, 2015, p. 35). The success of the image campaign was firstly the result of linking with another brand, seen by many as a cult brand— Apple. Secondly, it was significant that users were given access to a free application and with it the ability to share their achievements, which helped build a community around the brand.

APPARENT TRENDS AND PREDICTIONS FOR THE FUTURE

The above examples give reason to presume that the trend away from traditional branding and toward e-branding will continue. Traditional image campaigns on television, in the press or on the radio are not able to attract the attention of Generations Y and Z. This is mainly associated with the fact that Generations Y and Z are focused on new technologies and, moreover, Generation Z does not remember times before the Internet. It is the basic medium through which they gather information about the world.

It seems that within e-branding itself, the trend toward the use of mobile advertising directed to smartphone and tablet users will grow stronger. The amount of time consumers spend using these devices is growing every year, and mobile advertising can reach them at any time—while watching shows, taking public transit or shopping.

E-branding also provides great possibilities for forming individual relationships with customers, which will be of considerable significance when Generation Z, which expects personalized messages, comes to dominate the market.

BRAND CREATION IN SOCIAL MEDIA

The most important level in the development of a brand on the Internet is the ability to form a community around it, regardless of whether it is the brand of an organization, a product or a personal brand. Social media will play a key role in this.

The number of users of the largest global services is growing continuously, and new Internet sites constantly appear that form communities around them. As an example, one might give the number of active users of Facebook, the most popular service in the world that can be considered to be social media. In September 2012, this number exceeded 1 billion (Brzozowska-Woś, 2013, p. 56), and in September 2015 1.6 billion.

Research conducted by the Think Kong agency show that ca. 65% of respondents create and publish their own content on the Web, and up to 85% share content online. Web users also actively comment on and evaluate content placed on the Web by other users. Doing so on a daily basis was declared by 6% of those surveyed (Brzozowska-Woś, 2013, p. 57).

Organizations also take the opportunity to use social media to create brand image. The greatest popularity in this regard is enjoyed by Facebook (86% already are on the service, 8% plan to be), YouTube (36% are on, 13% plan to be), LinkedIn (30% are on, 13% plan to be), Goldenline.pl (20% are on, 11% plan to be), Google+ (23% are on, 21% plan to be), Twitter.com (18% are on, 10% plan to be), as well as blogs (20% own one, 20% plan to) (Brzozowska-Woś, 2013, pp. 58–59).

Facebook

Currently, the most popular social medium is Facebook, founded in 2004 by Harvard University student Mark Zuckerberg, who was named Person of the Year in 2010 by *Time* magazine. At first, the service focused on Harvard students, and gradually became widely accessible. The popularity of Facebook grew strikingly—in 2011, the number of users across the world was already 800 million (Polasik, Piotrowska, & Kunkowski, 2012, p. 251); in January 2014, around 1 billion (Motyka, 2012); by September 2015, the number of active Facebook users reached 1.59 billion. Every month, over 1 billion photos and 10 million videos are posted, of which there are currently 265 billion (Constine, 2016). The average user age is 22 years (Motyka, 2012).

On the service, registered users can create networks and groups, share messages and pictures, and can use the mobile application. Facebook allows creation of private profiles, but also fanpages of organizations, places and so on.

Currently, the most popular Facebook profiles belong to:

1. Facebook for Every Phone (590.96 million likes),
2. Facebook (170.72 million likes),
3. Cristiano Ronaldo (110.81 million likes),

4. Shakira (104.54 million likes),
5. Vin Diesel (98.48 million likes) (Statista.com).

Facebook allows for the creation of a personal brand profile, as well as the ability to reach potential viewers through appropriately profiled advertising. By posting attractive content, it is possible to build the engagement of viewers using interactive, two-way communication.

Twitter

Twitter works like a microblog, which allows users to exchange information using short, messages, limited to 140 characters, called tweets. Every registered user can send and read tweets. Twitter allows tagging and responding to others. Users can write messages on their profile via the Web, by text message or through a mobile app ("Twitter", n.d.). In May 2015, the service had over 500 million users, of whom over 332 million were active users ("Twitter", n.d.). Every day, 50 million users log in to the service, and every week over 1 billion messages appear (Polasik et al., 2012, p. 251).

The Pew Research Center in the United States reports that Twitter users declare a desire to be up to date with current events and to interact with interesting public figures. The ability to make comments or participate in discussions taking place in real time is also significant (Majchrzyk, 2015). Twitter's format makes it possible to rapidly transmit information that is later explored by politicians, journalists and other specialists.

As statistical data show, Polish Twitter users are predominantly men, with professional qualifications or who are retired, and this group makes up over 20% of users of the service. Equally active (as their numbers make up 60% of users) are school and university students using Twitter from large cities, members of free professions, journalists and company management (Majchrzyk, 2015).

In 2016, the most popular profiles, that is, followed by the largest number of users, belonged to:

1. Katy Perry (69.4 million)
2. Justin Bieber (63.3 million)
3. Barack Obama (58.9 million)
4. Taylor Swift (57.2 million)
5. YouTube (50.6 million)

6. Lady Gaga (46.3 million)
7. Justin Timberlake (45.1 million)
8. Rihanna (45 million)
9. Ellen DeGeneres (43.1 million)
10. Britney Spears (41.7 million) (Berg, 2015).

Twitter allows creation of sponsored campaigns. These make it possible to reach a concrete group of people, for example, those who have conversations on a topic of interest to us, or those following a particular account.

Instagram

This social photo hosting site is linked with a mobile application with the same name which is available for Windows Phone, iOS and Android. Instagram allows users to take photos and videos, modify them, apply digital filters and to share them on various social media. A characteristic trait of the application until recently was posting photos in a square format, but since August 27, 2015, it has been possible to post photos and videos in other image formats.

In April 2012, the service was purchased by Facebook for around $1 billion. However, after some time there were changes in the terms of service that allowed the sale of users' photos to outside businesses, which resulted in the drop of the number of active users from 100 million in September 2012 to ca. 90 million in January 2013 ("Instagram", n.d.).

Instagram users are evenly divided among iPhone and Android users. Among users of the service, 68% are women, and it is used more frequently by individuals living in large cities. People over the age of 35 make up 90% of Instagram users; 24% of users use the service several times daily (Smith, 2014).

The most popular Instagram users are:

1. Selena Gomez (69.5 million)
2. Taylor Swift (69.3 million)
3. Kim Kardashian (63.7 million)
4. Ariana Grande (63.1 million)
5. Beyoncé Knowles (63.1 million)
6. Justin Bieber (51.6 million)
7. Kylie Jenner (54.4 million)
8. Cristiano Ronaldo (51.6 million)

9. Kendall Jenner (51.5 million)
10. Nicki Minaj (50.6 million) ("The ten most popular Instagram accounts in pictures", 2015).

Instagram is a useful tool for product placement, and also provides the ability to create thematic channels, for example, regarding travel, in which the main content is visual. Recently, there has been the additional capability of creating personalized advertisements based on a user's preferences. Advertisers on Instagram may use the Facebook database if they link their accounts on both services.

Pinterest

This social medium is devoted to gathering and organizing selected visual materials. Pinterest is one giant bulletin board, on which users can pin fragments of what they find on web pages. Through an installable extension, the service downloads pictures from an indicated page and publishes them on the board. The pinned materials can be liked, copied to another user's board, or commented on. The name Pinterest comes from two words—*pin* and *interest* ("Pinterest", n.d.). The service also makes it possible for visual artists to display their own work.

Globally, the service is most popular among women—in 2012, they made up 83% of registered users. The only exception to this is Great Britain, where 56% of users are men. The predominant age is 35–44 years. In 2013, Pinterest had 48.7 million users ("Pinterest", n.d.).

Snapchat

This mobile application, available on Android and iOS devices, allows users to send pictures, films and drawings to individual contacts or to many people simultaneously. Receivers see a message for a maximum of 10 seconds, after which it self-destructs. The application was created in September 2011 based on the work of two students at Stanford University, Evan Spiegel and Robert Murphy. Snapchat has 100 million active users daily (Tweney, 2015), and in November 2015, the number of snaps sent daily exceeded 6 billion (Matney, 2015).

The main group of Snapchat users are individuals aged from 13 to 23. After its first year, the number of users over age 40 has also grown. The service is most frequently used to send selfies, and 30% of snaps are sent to a group of recipients ("Snapchat", n.d.).

Snapchat makes regular communication with receivers possible, which builds a sense of a connection or of closeness. The short messages are playful in character, do not show extensive marketing content, and are not directly suited to the sale of products, but rather to building a brand image. There is also the ability in the application to place advertising material in specially designed attachments.

LinkedIn

This is a social medium specializing in professional and business contacts, started in 2002 and in service since May 2003. In October 2015, it had over 400 million users in over 200 countries, of whom ca. 25% are active users (Młynarczyk, 2016). Starting in 2015, most revenue to the service has come from the sale of access to user information to recruiters and sales specialists. Both private individuals and organizations can have a profile on LinkedIn. It serves particularly to form and maintain professional contacts, to present one's abilities, experience and credibility.

The LinkedIn page is visited by on average 1.1 million users a month in Poland. These are mainly specialists or members of free professions or students. The average age of LinkedIn users is 25–34, and one in three visitors lives in a city of over 500,000 residents. Forty-five percent of users have received higher education ("Kim są użytkownicy serwisu LinkedIn?", 2015).

POSSIBILITIES FOR BUILDING A PERSONAL BRAND IN SOCIAL MEDIA

Social media make it possible for a message to reach individuals interested in specific content, and support the process of sales of products using digital marketing. Social media offer great possibilities for creating campaigns using viral advertising. Viral marketing is based on Internet users independently distributing information about a company, service or products, and "lies in initiating the situation in which potential customers will share information on their own about the company, service or products among themselves" ("Jak projektować reklamy w e-biznesie?", 2011). An example of viral marketing may be fun or intriguing short films or advertising pictures (often stylized to look amateur), which Internet users send to each other.

Thanks to social media, it is possible to create a personal brand by promoting a concrete idea—attachment to an important social topic, working for a non-profit or dedication to a particular issue may cause a given person to be seen in a decidedly more positive light. Identification with a commendable idea helps transfer part of the feelings and associations that people have about that idea to oneself.

On the opposite end is creating a brand using so-called hates—hateful messages on the Internet. An example might be the Polish blogger Matka Kurka, who publicly attached Jurek Owsiak, accusing the administration of the Great Orchestra of Christmas Charity of using donations to the orchestra for private purposes. In this way, the blogger became a recognizable brand online.

On all social media, there is also the phenomenon of buying followers with the purpose of creating an image—a larger number of fans, even paid ones, builds greater credibility according to the theory of social proof known from social psychology.

YouTube as an Environment that Creates the Possibility for Shaping a Personal Brand

Only 10 years old, YouTube ("YouTube w Polsce w 2014 roku", 2014) is clearly disrupting the model of how the media function and is becoming a new symbol of their power, replacing television. In a relatively short time, YouTube has become one of the strongest competitors for traditionally understood television. Currently, a growing number of YouTube users, especially younger ones, declare that they do not watch television—according to research by the Think Kong agency, there are 2.3 million of them in Poland ("YouTube w Polsce w 2014 roku", 2014). This implies big changes for the advertising market or for the distribution of information. In this context, YouTube has also become an important tool for creating a personal brand.

This is, above all, because films on the Internet have one of the highest indicators of conversion and are most effective at riveting the attention of receivers. Video leads to increasing engagement—research suggests that 65% of people watch at least 75% of a video they open. (DeMers, 2015). Video also creates the best opportunities for storytelling, which is a highly effective tool for creating an image.

One can state that YouTube is a democratic tool, allowing everyone who is interested to create and publish material, and at the same time thanks to the earnings from advertising and finding partners, it allows creators to gradually professionalize their activities. Thanks to YouTube, it is possible for messages to reach everywhere in an extremely short time and for their creators to retain full control over the content of these messages.

NOTES

1. Interesting research results regarding the behavior of Polish e-consumers compared to that of e-consumers in other countries can be found in Jaciow and Wolny (2011), and Jaciow, Solecka-Makowska, and Wolny (2013).
2. Research conducted by Palmieri and Lee (2015) shows that in 2010–2014 the number of viewers of the four main television networks dropped by 21% among those 18–49 years of age.
3. This is known as viral marketing.

REFERENCES

'Nie składałem ślubów ubóstwa.' Twardocha spór o luksusowe auto. (2015, July 3). *TVN24*. Retrieved from http://www.tvn24.pl/kultura-styl,8/szczepan-twardoch-zostal-ambasadorem-marki-mercedes-benz,557072.html

10 sekstaśm, którymi ekscytował się cały świat. (2014, April 9). Retrieved from http://joemonster.org/art/27273

Awdziej, M., & Tkaczyk, J. (2002). Wspieranie produktu wizerunkiem gwiazdy. *Marketing w Praktyce, 9.* Retrieved from http://rynkologia.pl/wp-content/uploads/2012/01/celebrity.pdf

Berg, M. (2015, June 29). The social 100: Twitter's most followed celebrities. *Forbes.* Retrieved from http://www.forbes.com/sites/maddieberg/2015/06/29/twitters-most-followed-celebrities-retweets-dont-always-mean-dollars/#636c62a37ef3

Boorstin, D. J. (1964). *The image: A guide to pseudo-events in America.* New York: Harper & Row.

Brzozowska-Woś, M. (2013). Media społecznościowe a wizerunek marki. *Journal of Management and Finance, 11*(1/1), 53–65.

Calzedonia chooses Julia Roberts as brand ambassador once more. (2015, October 16). *Fashion Network.* Retrieved from http://us.fashionmag.com/news/Calzedonia-chooses-Julia-Roberts-as-brand-ambassador-once-more,583750.html

CBOS. (2014, June). Internauci 2014. Komunikat z badań CBOS No. 82/2014. Retrieved from http://www.cbos.pl/SPISKOM.POL/2014/K_082_14.PDF

Constine, J. (2016, January 27). *Facebook climbs to 1.59 billion users and crushes Q4 estimates with $5.8B revenue.* Retrieved from http://techcrunch.com/2016/01/27/facebook-earnings-q4-2015

DeMers, J. (2015, July 23). 10 reasons your brand needs to be on YouTube. *Forbes.* Retrieved from http://www.forbes.com/sites/jay-sondemers/2015/07/23/10-reasons-your-brand-needs-to-be-on-youtube/#4cefccc235a0

Dołhasz, M. (2009). Celebrity Endorsement w działaniach reklamowych polskich przedsiębiorstw. In D. Surówka-Marszałek (Ed.), *Marketing.* Kraków, Poland: Krakowska Akademia im. Andrzeja Frycza Modrzewskiego.

Dziekoński, M. (2014). Marketing 3.0. In J. Królewski & P. Sala (Eds.), *E-marketing* (pp. 18–38). Warsaw, Poland: Wydawnictwo Naukowe PWN.

Gemius. (2015). *E-commerce w Polsce 2015. Gemius dla e-Commerce Polska* [research report]. Retrieved from https://www.gemius.pl/files/reports/E-commerce-w-Polsce-2015.pdf

Godzic, W. (2012). "Money listens" kontra "money speaks", czyli jak celebryci komunikują się z nami (jeśli się komunikują). In E. Kulczycki & M. Wendland (Eds.), *Komunikologia. Teoria i praktyka komunikacji* (pp. 31–51). Poznań: Wydawnictwo Naukowe Instytutu Filozofii UAM.

Gołąb-Andrzejak, E. (2014). Lojalność w społeczeństwie informacyjnym na przykładzie "pokolenia Milenium". *Marketing i Rynek, 11,* 11–21.

Goldman, D. (2012, March 24). *TOP 10 największych marek perfum gwiazd.* Retrieved from http://www.olfaktoria.pl/2012/03/top-10-najwiekszych-marek-perfum-gwiazd

Gruchoła, M., & Kruczek, E. (2013). Elementy wizerunku medialnego w internetowych serwisach plotkarskich w świetle badań ankietowych. *Rozprawy Społeczne, 1(7),* 137–156.

Guzek, D. (2012). Celebryci i ich medialna moralność. *Studia Socialia Cracoviensia, 4(2),* 117–127.

Howe, N., & Strauss, W. (1993). *13th gen: Abort, retry, ignore, fail?* New York: Vintage Books.

Instagram. (n.d.). *Wikipedia.* Retrieved April 11, 2016, from https://pl.wikipedia.org/wiki/Instagram

Jaciow, M., Stolecka-Makowska, A., & Wolny, R. (2013). *E-konsument w Europie. Komparatywna analiza zachowań.* Gliwice, Poland: Wydawnictwo Onepress.

Jaciow, M., & Wolny, R. (2011). *Polski e-konsument. Typologia, zachowania.* Gliwice, Poland: Wydawnictwo Onepress.

Jak projektować reklamy w e-biznesie?. (2011, November 29). Retrieved from http://prnews.pl/marketing-i-pr/jak-projektowac-reklamy-w-e-biznesie-66846.html

Joanna Krupa przeciwko hodowli zwierząt na futra w Polsce. (2015, December 10). Retrieved from http://ulicaekologiczna.pl/inspiracje/joanna-krupa-przeciwko-hodowli-zwierzat-na-futra-w-polsce

Kall, J. (2015). *Branding na smartfonie. Komunikacja mobilna marki*. Warsaw, Poland: Wolters Kluwer.

Kasperek, K. (2014). Książki celebrytów, czyli pisarze, gwiazdy i literatura. *Śląskie Studia Polonistyczne, 5*, 69–83.

Kaznowski, D. (2014). Social media – społeczny wymiar Internetu. In J. Królewski & P. Sala (Eds.), *E-marketing* (pp. 81–103). Warsaw, Poland: Wydawnictwo Naukowe PWN.

Kiefaber, D. (2013, June 7). *IBM's outdoor ads actually try to be useful and make cities better*. Retrieved from http://www.adweek.com/adfreak/ibms-outdoor-ads-actually-try-be-useful-and-make-cities-better-150091

Kim są użytkownicy serwisu LinkedIn?. (2015, December 9). Retrieved from https://www.gemius.pl/agencje-aktualnosci/kim-sa-uzytkownicy-serwisu-linkedin.html

Kolejna prowokacja Miley Cyrus – media aż huczą! (2015, November 23). Retrieved from http://www.viva-tv.pl/newsy/83220-kolejna-prowokacja-miley-cyrus-media-az-hucza

Królewski, J., & Sala, P. (Eds.). (2014). *E-marketing. Współczesne trendy. Pakiet startowy*. Warsaw, Poland: Wydawnictwo Naukowe PWN.

Madonna: dziewczyna, którą gwiazda rozebrała na koncercie, przyszła na kolejne show! Zobacz video! (2016, March 22). Retrieved from http://www.eska.pl/hotplota/news/madonna-dziewczyna-ktora-gwiazda-rozebrala-na-koncercie-przyszla-na-kolejne-show-zobacz-video/n/92639

Madonna zabawia się krzyżem. (2010, May 6). Retrieved from http://www.se.pl/rozrywka/gwiazdy/madonna-zabawia-sie-krzyzem_138365.html

Majchrzyk, L. (2015, November 7). *Kim są użytkownicy Facebooka i Twittera w Polsce?* Retrieved from https://mobirank.pl/2015/11/07/kim-sa-uzytkownicy-facebooka-i-twittera-w-polsce

Marshall, P. D. (1997). *Celebrity and power: Fame in contemporary culture*. Minneapolis, MN: University of Minnesota Press.

Matney, L. (2015, November 9). *Snapchat reaches 6 billion daily videos views, tripling from 2 billion in May*. Retrieved from http://techcrunch.com/2015/11/09/snapchat-reaches-6-billion-daily-videos-views-tripling-from-2-in-may

Mazurkiewicz, B. (2014). Rola liderów opinii w komunikacji nieformalnej. *Marketing i Rynek, 11*, 31–39.

McCrindle, M. & Hooper, D. (2007). *Generation Y. Attracting, engaging and leading a new generation at work*. http://avpma.ava.com.au/sites/default/files/AVPMA_website/resources/5.2%20Generation%20Y%20-%20Attracting,%20Engaging%20%26%20Leading%20a%20New%20Generation%20at%20Work.pdf

Młynarczyk, K. (2016, January 7). *Linkedin – podsumowanie kierunków rozwoju serwisu w 2015*. Retrieved from http://socjomania.pl/linkedin-podsumowanie-roku-2015

Motyka, A. (2012, October 4). *Facebookowi nie straszne konta-widma. Zuckerberg ma już miliard!* Retrieved from http://media2.pl/internet/96698-Facebooko wi-nie-straszne-konta-widma.-Zuckerberg-ma-juz-miliard.html

Mróz, B. (2013). *Konsument w globalnej gospodarce. Trzy perspektywy*. Warsaw, Poland: Oficyna Wydawnicza Szkoły Głównej Handlowej w Warszawie.

Olczyk, T. (2013). Teoria i praktyka celebrytyzacji politycznej. *Celebryci polityczni w internetowych serwisach plotkarskich, Środkowoeuropejskie Studia Polityczne, 1,* 71–90.

Online branding – potrzeba nowych strategii. (n.d.). Retrieved from http://www. migomedia.pl/online-branding-potrzeba-nowych-strategii

Opel rozpoczyna jedyną w swoim rodzaju kampanię i konkurs #ADAMYOURSELF: 'Morze możliwości – dokładnie mój styl. (2015, August 12). [Press release]. Retrieved from http://www.opel.pl/poznaj-opla/o-oplu/ opel-aktualnosci/2015/grudzien/adam-yourself.html

Palmeri, C., & Lee, E. (2015, May 15). TV networks bank on a miniseries revival. *Bloomberg Business*. Retrieved from http://www.bloomberg.com/bw/article s/2014-05-15/tv-networks-fight-netflix-with-miniseries-revival

Parris, J. A. (2010, January–February). Is your self-service Millennial friendly? *Speech Technology*. Retrieved from http://www.speechtechmag.com/Articles/Column /Inside-Outsourcing/Is-Your-Self-Service-Millennial-Friendly-60407.aspx

Paul, P. (2001). Getting inside Gen Y. *American Demographics, 23*(9), 42–49.

Pinterest. (n.d.). *Wikipedia*. Retrieved April 11, 2016, from https://pl.wikipedia. org/wiki/Pinterest

Podgórska, J. (2014, February 12). Niewinny Nergal. *Polityka*. Retrieved from http://www.polityka.pl/tygodnikpolityka/kraj/1570431,1,nergal-podarl-biblie-ale-nie-obrazil-uczuc-religij-nych-jest-prawomocny-wyrok.read

Polasik, M., Piotrowska, A., & Kunkowski, J. (2012). Wykorzystanie serwisów społecznościowych w polskim handlu elektronicznym, *Zeszyty Naukowe. Studia Informatica. Uniwersytet Szczeciński, 29,* 249–262.

Połowianiuk, M. (2015, July). *Telewizja nie ma przyszłości*. Retrieved from http:// www.spidersweb.pl/2015/07/telewizja-nie-ma-przy-szlosci.html

Polski rynek reklamy będzie rósł. (2014, September 23). Retrieved from http:// brief.pl/wiedza/polski_rynek_reklamy_bedzie_rosl/

Raport IGRZ o wynikach reklamy OOH w Polsce w roku 2014. (2015, January). [annual report]. Retrieved from http://igrz.home.pl/Raporty/2014% 20RAPORT%20ROCZNY%20IGRZ.pdf

Raport na temat wartości polskiego rynku e-commerce w 2015 roku. (n.d.). Retrieved from http://obserwatoriumit.pl/aktualnosci/raport-na-temat-warto sci-polskiego-rynku-e-commerce-w-2015-roku

Roszkowski, J. (2013). Monitoring mediów społecznościowych. In J. Królewski & P. Sala (Eds.), *E-marketing* (pp. 336–373). Warsaw: Wydawnictwo Naukowe PWN.

Sinha, S. (2012, March 8). Top 10 most popular celeb brand ambassadors in the world (PHOTOS). *International Business Times.* Retrieved from http://www.ib times.com/top-10-most-popular-celebbrand-ambassadors-world-photos-554575

Smith, C. (2014, July 17). *Here's why Instagram's demographics are so attractive to brands.* Retrieved from http://www.businessinsider.com/instagram-demogra phics-2013-12

Snapchat. (n.d.). *Wikipedia.* Retrieved April 11, 2016, from https://en.wikipedia. org/wiki/Snapchat#cite_ref-8

Sosin, N. (2014). Wizyta u barbarzyńskiego golibrody Nergal: Dbanie o atrybuty męskości ma wpływ na to, co mamy wewnątrz. Retrieved from http://weekend. gazeta.pl/weekend/1,152121,16856499,Wizyta_u_barbarzynskiego_golibrod y__Nergal__Dbanie.html

Statista.com. (n.d.). Retrieved from http://www.statista.com/statistics/269304/ international-brands-on-facebook-by-number-of-fans

Surmacz, T. (2014). Rynek internetowy w Polsce i na świecie. In J. Królewski & P. Sala (Eds.), *E-marketing* (pp. 39–63). Warsaw, Poland: Wydawnictwo Naukowe PWN.

Szylar, M. (2015). Rok 2015 częścią Ery Mobile. In *E-commerce w Polsce 2015. Gemius dla e-Commerce Polska* (pp. 173–174). Retrieved from https://www. gemius.pl/files/reports/E-commerce-w-Polsce-2015.pdf

The ten most popular Instagram accounts in pictures. (2015, December 14). Retrieved from http://www.telegraph.co.uk/technology/2015/12/14/the-ten-most-popular-instagram-accounts-in-pictures

Thomas, G. M. (2004). Building the buzz in the hive mind. *Journal of Consumer Behaviour, 4,* 64–72.

Trzeciak, S. (2015). *Wizerunek publiczny w internecie. Kim jesteś w sieci?* Gliwice, Poland: Helion.

Tweney, D. (2015, May 26). *Engagement to die for: Snapchat has 100M daily users, 65% of whom upload photos.* Retrieved from http://venturebeat.com /2015/05/26/snapchat-has-100m-daily-users-65-of-whom-upload-photos

Twitter. (n.d.). *Wikipedia.* Retrieved April 11, 2016, from https://pl.wikipedia.org/ wiki/Twitter

UNICEF. (n.d.). *UNICEF people.* Retrieved from http://www.unicef.org/people/ people_ambassadors_international.html

van den Bergh, J., & Behrer, M. (2012). *Jak kreować marki, które pokocha pokolenie Y?* Warsaw, Poland: Samo Sedno Edgard.

Williams, K. C., & Page, R. A. (2011). Marketing to the generations. *Journal of Behavioral Studies in Business.* Retrieved from http://www.aabri.com/manuscri pts/10575.pdf

Wojewódzki i Figurski ponownie ukarani za rasizm, Eska Rock musi zapłacić 50 tys. zł. (2012, April 3). *Gazeta.pl*. Retrieved from http://wiadomosci.gazeta.pl/ wiadomosci/1,114873,11471198,Wojewodzki_i_Figurski_ponownie_ukarani_ za_rasizm_.html

YouTube w Polsce w 2014 roku. (2014, October 8). Retrieved from http://www. brief.pl/artykul,2330,youtube_w_polsce_w_2014_roku.html

Personal Branding on YouTube in the United States and in Poland: Comparative Analysis Based on Academic Literature and Published Marketing Studies

Abstract This chapter addresses the question of personal branding on YouTube, and constitutes an attempt at a comparative analysis of the ways this social medium is used to shape personal brands in Poland and in the United States. This chapter characterizes the cultural and technological conditions that determine personal branding strategies in each country, and the main ways in which shaping a personal brand is changing in Poland and in the United States.

Keywords YouTube branding • Social media • Cultural differences • Branding strategies

THE REACH OF YOUTUBE IN THE UNITED STATES AND IN POLAND: CURRENT SITUATION

The Social Medium YouTube: General Statistics

Around the world, over 1 billion people use YouTube—that is nearly one in three individuals who use the Internet. The number of viewers aged from 18 to 45 and from 18 to 49 who watch YouTube, even if one only counts those using the mobile version of the service, is greater than for any cable television channel in the United States. The number of hours that viewers

© The Author(s) 2018
M. Grzesiak, *Personal Brand Creation in the Digital Age*,
https://doi.org/10.1007/978-3-319-69697-3_4

spend watching videos (and so the total watching time) grew in 2015 by 60% over the previous year—the highest growth in two years. The number of individuals watching videos daily on YouTube grew by 40% for the year. The number of users who start watching videos from the YouTube main page—as if they were turning on the television—grew over three times over the previous year ("YouTube dla prasy", n.d.).

The popularity of the service is growing constantly; over the course of eight years the average monthly interest in the service grew four times—from 19% in 2008 to 73% in 2014 ("Czterokrotny wzrost liczby użytkowników", 2015). The speed of the growth of the total time spent viewing content on YouTube increased as well. This time grows by 50% every year, and this has been the case now for three years ("YouTube dla prasy", n.d.).

Mobile Devices

As data from the service show, viewers are spending a growing amount of time watching videos on YouTube during each visit. On mobile devices, the average length of a viewing session is now over 40 minutes, which signifies a growth of over 50% for the year. The number of hours spent by users watching videos on YouTube on mobile devices grew by 100% over the year. Over half of all views on YouTube are on mobile devices. Revenue from views on mobile devices doubled in 2015 ("YouTube dla prasy", n.d.).

Advertising

Revenues from service partners are growing by 50% a year and this dynamic growth has been continuing for three years. The number of channels that produce six-figure annual revenues (in US dollars) grew by 50% in 2015. The number of advertisers that place video advertisements on the service grew by over 40% for the year. For the 100 largest advertisers, the average amount spent per advertiser grew by over 60% for the year ("YouTube dla prasy", n.d.).

Reach of YouTube in the United States

In the United States, 66.4% of Internet users access YouTube at least once a week, which puts it in second place among social media—only Facebook is more popular, which is used by 76.8% of Internet users in the United States ("Snapchat's audience is teen-y", 2014). YouTube is most popular among the youngest group of users; if the age of Internet users is taken into account, the percentage of people using YouTube is as follows:

(a) among those aged 14–17—81.9%
(b) among those aged 18–34—77.6%
(c) among those aged 35–54—54.2% ("Snapchat's audience is teen-y", 2014).

Research conducted in 2013 shows that 58.2% of Internet users in the United States have an account on YouTube ("Percentage of U.S. internet users", 2013). Moreover, 18.4% of YouTube users have at least two favorite channels which they watch regularly ("Do you have any favorite YouTube channels", n.d.). In mid-2015, around 50% of mobile device users in the United States accessed YouTube with a smartphone or tablet. That same year, research showed that YouTube was one of the most popular places where mobile device users looked for specific videos ("Statistics and facts about YouTube", n.d.).

Reach of YouTube in Poland

In 2015, YouTube was in third place in terms of the number of monthly site visitors in Poland (Szewczyk Ł., 2015). The figure in April 2015 was 16,370,495 users. First place in this ranking was the Google group, with 20,585,722 visitors, and second was Facebook with 17,314,530 site visitors in Poland.

Moreover, the most recent statistics indicate that in the category of real users (RU), in other words, the estimated number of people visiting the page of a given service, regardless of whether they are registered users, YouTube was visited by 8.28 million men and 8.09 million women. Among men, the number of users in specific age categories is as follows:

(a) 7–14 years—926,092
(b) 15–24 years—1,625,709
(c) 25–34 years—2,077,837
(d) 35–44 years—1,605,815
(e) 45–54 years—1,138,185
(f) 55 or more years—907,573 users ("YouTube Trends", 2015).

For women, the number of users of YouTube in specific age categories is as follows:

(a) 7–14 years—929,679
(b) 15–24 years—2,182,896
(c) 25–34 years—2,136,654
(d) 35–44 years—1,392,410
(e) 45–54 years—806,764
(f) 55 or more years—640,881 ("YouTube Trends", 2015).

The above statistics show that female viewers are younger than males, and the greatest difference in this regard—at 26%—is visible in the 15–25 age category.

Currently, 72% of Internet users in Poland use YouTube. Research conducted in 2014 by the Polish Interaktywny Instytut Badań Rynkowych [Interactive Market Research Institute] shows that 45% of those studied spend more time watching video on YouTube than watching television, and 20% spent the same amount of time. In addition, YouTube has a near monopoly in Poland: 67% of those studied watch video on this service, and on others, including VOD or news services, only a bit over 20%. The largest group of individuals watch music videos on YouTube (75%), in second place are comedy (66%), next DYI (37%), and culinary (25%) videos (Gwóźdź, 2014). Among those studied, 38% subscribe to favorite channels; 16% follow 1–2 favorites, 22% 6–10 channels, 19% 11–25 channels, 3% 26–50 channels, and 9% of individuals follow more than 50 channels. Subscribers are most frequently young people (the highest percentage of subscribers, 62%, is aged 15–24). Among individuals aged 25–34, 38% are YouTube subscribers, in the 25–49 age group, 15%, and among those over 50, 16%. These are more often men than women (46% of men and 29% of women subscribe) (Miotk, 2014).

LEADERS IN THE TREND TOWARD SHAPING A PERSONAL BRAND USING YOUTUBE

The Most Popular YouTube Channels in the World

The most popular YouTube channels in the world (excluding Vivo music streaming channels; as of March 10, 2016) are shown in Table 4.1 below ("List of the most subscribed users", n.d.).

Table 4.1 Most popular YouTube channels in the world

Channel name	Owner	Country	Number of subscribers	Content type
PewDiePie	Felix Kjellberg	Sweden	43 million	Video games
HolaSoyGerman	Germán Garmendia	Chile	27 million	vlogs
YouTube Spotlight	YouTube, Inc.	USA	24 million	Entertainment
Smosh	Ian Hecox, Anthony Padilla	USA	21 million	Sketches
elrubiusOMG	Rubén Doblas Gundersen	Spain	17 million	Video games
Nigahiga	Ryan Higa, Sean Fujiyoshi	USA	16 million	Comedy
VanossGaming	Evan Fong	Canada	16 million	Video games
JennaMarbles	Jenna Mourey	USA	15 million	vlogs

Source: Own elaboration based on available data on YouTube

First on the list is Felix Kjellberg, who appears on YouTube under the pseudonym **PewDiePie**, and at present is the highest-earning YouTuber in the world. In 2014, he earned $7.4 million from advertisements displayed along with his films on YouTube. Last year, it was already $12 million. Most of the videos he posts are what are called Let's Plays—a recording showing computer game play. Kjellberg enriches this with his peculiar and characteristic running commentary. That he speaks in English and not his native language has helped to create his popularity and opened the doors to international fame. PewDiePie started his channel near the end of 2010. Since then, his videos have had over 9 billion views. Currently, Kjellberg publishes through his partner network, Maker Studios, which was bought last year by Disney ("7,4 mln dol. w rok", 2015).

HolaSoyGerman, or Germán Alejandro Garmendia Aranis, is a Chilean musician, singer, writer and comedian. He has produced a number of songs with his band, all of which are available on his YouTube channel. His book, *Chupa el Perro*, appeared on April 28, 2016 ("Germán Garmendia", n.d.)

YouTube Spotlight is the official channel of the YouTube service on which various videos and events are published. In addition, YouTube Nation and annual YouTube Rewind videos appear on this channel ("YouTube spotlight", n.d.)

Smosh is an American comedy duet, made up of Ian Hecox (born November 30, 1987 in Sacramento) and Anthony Padilla (born September

16, 1987 also in Sacramento). They began in 2003 when Padilla began to post videos on the Newgrounds website under the name Smosh. Soon his childhood friend, Ian Hecox joined him, and they began to post videos on their YouTube channel, which quickly rose to be one of the most popular. They earned $8.5 from their work in 2015 ("Najlepiej zarabiający youtuberzy na świecie", 2015).

Rubén Doblas Gundersen, or **elrubiusOMG**, is a Spanish YouTuber, whose channel is devoted to gaming. Currently, the channel is fourth in terms of number of global subscriptions and, moreover, it is the number two Spanish-language channel, and number one in Spain. El Rubius' first video on YouTube was posted in 2006 and, since 2011, he has been pursuing a YouTube career exclusively. Before that, he posted only occasionally. In 2014, he appeared in a minor role in the Spanish film *Torrente 5*, directed by Santiago Segura ("El Rubius", n.d.).

The channel **nigahiga** was started on July 20, 2006 by Ryan Higa, Sean Fujiyoshi, Tim Enos and Tarynn Nago, known together as The Yabo Crew. According to Higa, the name of the channel is a combination of the word *niga*, which means "rant" in Japanese, together with his last name. The videos that Higa posts are comedy ("Ryan Higa", n.d.).

Evan Fong, whose online pseudonym is **VanossGaming**, is a Canadian video game commentator. The videos he posts on YouTube focus on games played with a few of his friends. They have to do with completing concrete tasks in games and working through particular levels, but also have a comedy character. Since Fong began his YouTube channel in 2011, he has gained more that 16 million subscribers, and his videos have received more than 4 billion views ("VanossGaming", n.d.).

JennaMarbles, or Jenna N. Mourey, is an American YouTuber, actress and comedian. Her channel is followed by over 15 million YouTube users, which means that she is seventh on the list of most popular YouTubers and is the highest ranked woman on the list. In 2010, Marbles published the video *How to Trick People into Thinking You're Good Looking*, which in the first week received 3.5 million views. The video, *How to Avoid Talking to People You Don't Want to Talk to*, was cited by the *New York Times* and ABC News. The YouTuber posts videos once a week, which have received a total of over 1.8 billion views ("Jenna Marbles", n.d.).

Most Popular YouTube Channels in Poland

The list of YouTubers who, as of August 2015, had gained the largest number of subscriptions is shown in Table 4.2 below.[1]

In Table 4.2 above, it is worth noting that the first six places among the most popular channels belong to ones created after 2010, and so after YouTube had been operating on the market for at least five years, had an established position and the possibilities that it offered were already widely known. On the one hand, this shows that the greatest potential for rapid growth belonged to those channels with topics in accord with the latest trends or the most current expectations of users. On the other hand, one can conclude that YouTube makes it possible to reach an audience of millions in a relatively short time.

The list of the ten most popular channels in Poland also shows what content categories currently attract the greatest number of users. These are primarily entertainment channels, offering material related to pranking or lifehacking, but also music channels and gaming channels devoted to reviews of computer games. It can be estimated that channels in the following categories currently enjoy the greatest popularity: entertainment, games, education, cooking, fashion and beauty, lifestyle, sports and technology ("YouTube Trends", 2015). Of these, the leading places in the ranking of viewership belong to:

Entertainment:

1. SA Wardega—3.2 million subscribers
2. Abstarchuje—1.77 million subscribers
3. 5 Sposobów na...—1.36 million subscribers.

Games:

1. reZigiusz—1.55 million subscribers
2. Stuu Games—1.45 million subscribers
3. Blowek—1.33 million subscribers.

Education:

1. SciFun—540 million subscribers
2. MaturaToBzdura.TV—370 thousand subscribers
3. Historia bez cenzury—200 thousand subscribers.

Table 4.2 Most popular YouTube channels in Poland

Channel name	Subscriptions	Views	Type of content	Date channel started
SA Wardega	3,230,261	514,488,118	Entertainment (pranking[a])	January 30, 2012
AbstrachujeTV	1,774,582	266,024,307	Entertainment	October 4, 2012
reZigiusz	1,550,180	274,365,627	Gaming	August 27, 2012
Stuu games	1,451,148	263,118,230	Gaming	October 5, 2012
5 Sposobów na...	1,360,938	179,863,615	Entertainment (lifehacking[b])	July 3, 2013
Blowek	1,339,736	230,582,994	Gaming	April 13, 2011
Niekryty Krytyk	1,221,700	185,662,016	Game, book and film reviews	December 9, 2006
Step records	1,202,684	818,809,797	Entertainment (music)	January 4, 2009
skkf	1,147,290	181,509,020	Gaming	July 27, 2006
ProstoTV	1,061,329	796,522,207	Entertainment (music)	January 18, 2008

Source: Own elaboration based on available data on YouTube
[a]Pranking, meaning here video content based on pre-arranged surprising situations and recording the reactions of unwitting participants in it
[b]Lifehacking, meaning here video content based on presenting simple ways of managing domestic, everyday tasks

Cooking:

1. paei100–490 thousand subscribers
2. SkutecznieTv—70 thousand subscribers
3. Kotlet.TV—60 thousand subscribers.

Fashion and beauty:

1. Red Lipstick Monster—40 thousand subscribers
2. stylizacjeTV—30 thousand subscribers
3. littlemooonster96–20 thousand subscribers ("YouTube Trends", 2015).

It is important to remember, however, that YouTube is an interactive service, which means that for potential advertisers interested in a channel, the number of views or subscriptions is as important as the activity, as shown by the number of comments, on that channel. In this regard, the best results are achieved by the gaming channel Mandzio, with 75,497 comments. The next places are held by: reZigiusz—54,427 comments, Nolif—40,865 comments, IsAmUxPompa—37,671 comments, and Remigiusz Maciaszek—27,881 comments ("YouTube Trends", 2015). It should be added that all the top ten most commented on channels are in the gaming category.

Culturally Specific Elements in Shaping a Personal Brand on the American and the Polish Markets: Comparison

Personal branding is one of many phenomena that arose in the United States and migrated to Europe. It is thus not surprising that in the United States there is considerably more awareness of the need to create a personal brand than in Poland, where the view still prevails that the need to create a personal brand only applies to celebrities or politicians (Poczęsna, 2014).

Young people in the United States, over the course of their education, already grow familiar with elements that they can later use to create their personal brand—for example, at colleges and universities, and often in high schools there are classes in public speaking. The level of social acceptance of speaking about oneself as well as advertising one's abilities is also significantly higher. In Poland, the term "selling yourself" ("*sprzedawać siebie*") still has a negative overtone. Americans are more inclined to speak directly about themselves, without the fear of becoming a laughing stock.

In the United States, people from a greater number of industries and professions than in Poland are interested in topics related to shaping a personal brand. This is a result, as previously mentioned, of the longer tradition of personal branding in the American market than in the Polish one. There is also greater awareness of the possibilities offered by YouTube for shaping a personal brand. Americans use the service much more as a tool to promote products and services. It should be mentioned, however, that video promotion of local businesses has long been an element of the American market (advertising gas stations, small stores, car-rental agencies, bakeries and so on).

Consequently, the dynamically developing market for multi-channel network agencies working professionally to shape personal brands translates into greater competition among companies offering these services, as well as into greater advertising budgets.

The multicultural nature of American society, especially compared to Polish society, means that both the content published on YouTube as well as the audience are more diverse. Topics that are seen in Poland as taboo are also raised more often, and personal brands are built on that basis.

The dominance of English-language material in the world means that all kinds of creative people—actors, singers and even American YouTubers—immediately, as if in passing, reach a wider audience than local people creating their own brand in their local national market. Success achieved in the United States means recognizability around the world.

The only material that reaches a wider audience than recordings of people using English are those productions that use no language at all. An example might be the previously mentioned Sylwester Wardęga, whose film *Mutant Giant Spider Dog* was the most-viewed video on YouTube in 2014 (Gross, 2014).

However, American YouTubers still earn much more than their counterparts in other countries (Pająk, 2015)—among other things, this has to do with the entirely different costs, and thus the revenues from advertising in the United States and, for example, in Poland, as will be discussed in greater detail in the next chapter.

USE OF HIGH-TECH IN SHAPING A PERSONAL BRAND ON THE AMERICAN AND POLISH MARKETS

High-Tech: An Attempt at Definition

High-tech is a vernacular description for those technologies that are most advanced at a given moment ("High-tech", n.d.). It also applies to the most important technological developments of the last decade. In the past few years, companies based on the use of the latest technologies have been known as startups.

Equipment

Miniaturization of Video Cameras
Over the past 20 years, there has been a massive development in image recording technology. Most of all the size of video cameras has changed and, with that, their accessibility and the costs of production. That has had a direct effect on their wide availability on the market. For example, at the end

of the 1990s the most popular cameras were several dozen centimeters long and weighed several kilograms. Today, the GoPro Hero 3 sports camera is 40 mm long and weighs 70 g (Leniwiec, 2013). What is more, GoPro offers much greater image quality—the camera can record in full HD (1920 × 1080 pixels), whereas in the 1990s the standard was PAL quality (768 × 576 pixels).

Universality of Video Cameras
With the development of technology, video cameras became available to nearly every consumer. Today, it is not necessary to buy specialized hardware to be able to record images in high definition. The vast majority of cell phones (especially smartphones) now have lenses that allow for the recording of video in full HD quality, as well as photos in the professional RAW format (Duda, 2016). What is more, the clear majority of cameras, including SLRs, also offer the ability to record images in high quality. Many professionals use cameras that are widely available on the market (Niemycki, 2011).

Selfie Sticks
For several years, so-called selfie sticks have been growing in popularity—a kind of monopod extension for a smartphone for taking selfies (pictures of oneself) from sufficient distance to maintain a wide frame. With this device, photographs can have the characteristics of a selfie, that is, they are taken by the person in the picture, but allowing the background or other people to be seen, as if the picture were taken by a third person or using a timer. For several years, selfies have been one of the most popular types of content on social media, and so the introduction of selfie sticks was a response to existing user habits and behaviors (Szewczyk O., 2015). In some public spaces, the use of selfie sticks is prohibited, however (for example, in stadiums and museums) (Połowianiuk, 2014).

Popularity of Drones
To take an image corresponding to a traditional aerial photograph, an airplane is no longer needed. This role has been assumed by drones— unmanned, miniature airships to which video recording equipment can be attached. The introduction of drones to the market significantly lowered the cost of taking pictures from the air ("Zyskują coraz większą popularność", 2016). Drones for filming have between four and eight pairs of blades (the number affects image stability) as well as additional stabilization systems. A drone can be outfitted with any recording equipment, but usually cameras

with a video recording function are used. The operator piloting the drone from the ground can also view the image being recorded. All this results in continual growth in the market for drones. ("Zyskują coraz większą popularność", 2016).

Sports Micro Cameras
The next significant change in equipment was the appearance of sports micro cameras, which allow for the recording of sports activities. Their dominant trait is their small size, high durability, resistance to atmospheric conditions and moisture, low price and high image quality. These traits apply to cameras including the GoPro Hero, the most popular series of sports cameras whose name has become synonymous with all products of this type ("Poznaj najpopularniejsze produkty", 2016). These cameras allow low-cost recording during sports activities or vacations. Economists predict that, by no later than 2019, this market segment will grow rapidly (Seitz, 2015).

Smart TV
Smart TV technology makes it possible to browse the Internet with a television. In particular this applies to VOD (video on demand) services, as well as social media like YouTube (Bójko, 2014). Because of this, videos on the Internet can easily be watched on the television screen without the need to invest in additional hardware or to connect a notebook or PC every time. What is more, television manufacturers are developing a common smart TV interface which will make TV receivers compatible with different brands of smartphones and tablets ("Smart TV alliance", 2012). Thanks to this, smartphones and tablets can be used as wireless control devices.

Technology

Increase in Quality
The spread of video recording is also associated with a substantial increase in quality. At the end of the 90s, the most popular formats were PAL (768 × 576 pixels) and NTSC. Today, most smartphones record in full HD (1920 × 1080 pixels), and many cameras in 4 K format (4096 × 3112 or 4096 × 2160 pixels). With the growth of resolution there was also a growth in image stabilization systems, lossless zoom (digital and optical), as well as software for rapid video editing and mobile platforms. The first television broadcasts in 4 K resolution were also launched (Pieczonka, 2013).

Streaming Video
Streaming video is sending a video stream through the Internet. It takes place live (in real time), which distinguishes streaming from posting previously recorded films. Streaming is widely used in education (webinars, conference broadcasts), sports (sports broadcasts), business services (teleconferences), and entertainment (YouTubers), as well as to facilitate personal contacts (communicators with a streaming option, for example, Skype). What is more, streaming is becoming a convenient replacement for products that were previously downloaded by users from the net. An example might be the VOD service Netflix, which gives users streaming access to films and series. Expansion of this technology to computer games is also planned (Kamiński, 2013).

New Video Technologies
Over the past few years, a few new branches of film production have developed. These include filming in 360 degrees and virtual reality—VR. 360-degree video is made using specialized equipment (cameras), and editing requires dedicated software ("Filmy w technologii 360°", 2015). All of this incurs higher costs for such recording, and so currently the technique is used mainly by specialized agencies. 360-degree video is already available on YouTube (Ułan, 2015). In Poland, this technology was first used in the production of the video broadcast of the Orange Warsaw Festival ("Filmy w technologii 360°", 2015). VR is a recording technique that allows playback on special devices—VR goggles. With these, the viewer has the impression of being a participant in the recorded scene. Such images can be displayed both on the screens of VR goggles (connected to a computer or in conjunction with a smartphone) (Pisarski, 2015), and also on a computer monitor (the previously mentioned 360-degree tool on YouTube).

Mobile Applications
Along with the development of image recording technology, there has been an expansion of the mobile applications available for both recording videos as well as uploading them to the net. For recording videos, the popular communicator Snapchat is used, and video can be sent via Messenger as well. Social media applications (Facebook, Google+) also allow sharing video content with other users quickly. Another popular application is Vine, which allows users to record short videos of up to 6 seconds (Sippey, 2013).

Streaming is available, among other services, on Skype, (video chat, video conferences) as well as YouTube (webinars).

Payment Gateways
The rapid development of small online payments has made making money online much easier. There are several popular payment gateway providers using electronic banking or payment via credit card, including PayU and Przelewy24 in Poland. A separate tool is PayPal, which can be used like a pre-paid bank account. The services of payment gateways are widely available and can be used by individuals and businesses for sales of their goods and services (Kowalski, 2013).

ACTIVITY AS A YOUTUBER AS A SOURCE OF INCOME

Activity as a YouTuber as a Source of Income Worldwide

The most popular YouTubers in the world earn millions of dollars from their activity on their channel alone, thanks to the advertisements shown along with their videos.

Felix Kjellberg, who owns the PewDiePie channel on YouTube, is currently the highest-earning YouTuber in the world. In 2014, he earned $7.4 million from advertisements shown along with his videos, and in 2015 the figure was $12 million. He achieved this success by playing games and recording videos related to that activity. He reviews many productions on his channel, using funny, but also often vulgar, vocabulary. He started his channel in April 2010 and since then his videos have received over 9 billion views. Currently, PewDiePie has over 43 million subscribers ("Najlepiej zarabiający youtuberzy", 2015). Kjellberg looks to protect his privacy—he avoids interviews and conferences and only rarely appears at the California studios of YouTube (Domaradzki, 2015).

Smosh is a duet made up of Ian Hecox and Anthony Padilla, two childhood friends who currently run as many as five channels on YouTube. They present their own sketches, and a few months ago they made a feature-length film, *Smosh: The Movie*. Thanks to their activity on YouTube, they earned as much as $8.5 million, achieving the same level of success as the Fine Brothers ("Najlepiej zarabiający youtuberzy", 2015).

The Fine Brothers, two brothers, Benny and Rafi Fine, achieved popularity owing to a series of videos in which they showed the reactions of people watching videos on YouTube, including those of PewDiePie, or music videos of Nicki Minaj. The success they achieved online inspired the Fine Brothers and Nick Cannon to create the program *React to That*, which is broadcast on the children's channel Nickelodeon. The Fine Brothers have nearly 14 million subscribers and earn $8.5 million from their channel (Domaradzki, 2015).

Lindsey Stirling achieved popularity thanks to her unusual talent—she can play the violin and dance simultaneously. When her work did not suit the tastes of record producers, she decided to start her own YouTube channel. Since 2007, she has gained 7.8 million subscribers, and earned $6 million from advertising last year (Domaradzki, 2015).

Rhett & Link, that is, Rhett McLaughlin and Charles Lincoln Neal III, are one of the oldest on the list of the richest YouTubers, being 38 and 37 years old respectively. Both graduated from North Carolina State University and worked in corporate America for many years. Popularity came to them through parody of television morning news on the Good Mythical Morning channel. They earned $4.5 million last year from their channel (advertising brands such as Gillette, Toyota and Wendy's) (Domaradzki, 2015).

KSI, or Olajide Olatunji, began his Internet career much like PewDiePie, with a gaming channel on which he discussed video games. He decided, however, to use his popularity to launch a career in music. His hip-hop single, *Lamborghini* reached the UK Top 40 in April 2015. In September 2016, KSI had over 11 million subscribers and earned $4.5 million from his channel (Berg, 2015).

Channels on makeup, hairstyling or clothing constitute the largest share of popular videos on YouTube. Michelle Phan, who achieved fame by showing women how to put on makeup like the stars do, is currently the most popular YouTuber in this category. She earns an annual income of $3 million from her recordings ("Najlepiej zarabiający youtuberzy", 2015). Not only does she make money from her videos, but also from her own line of cosmetics and tips. She reinvests nearly all the money back into her enterprise.

Lilly Singh, appearing on YouTube as IISuperwomanII, is a comedian specializing in standup based on her Indian background. Singh is also a singer—in 2015, as part of her "A Trip to Unicorn Island" tour, she visited 27 cities around the world. Her earnings on YouTube are estimated at $2.5 million. Roman Atwood is a YouTuber who makes pranking videos, and his pranks are similar in concept to those of Polish YouTuber Sylwester Wardęga. Atwood is famed for his astonishing ideas, such as startling beach vacationers with an artificial skunk. His activities have attracted over 7 million subscribers, and his annual income is estimated at $2.5 million.

Rosanna Pansino operates a channel with instructional cooking and baking videos. In 2015, she also published a cookbook, *The Nerdy Nummies Cookbook: Sweet Treats for the Geek in All of Us*. Pansino earns money in part by working with Wilton Brands, a manufacturer of bakeware. Her channel has 5.9 million subscribers on YouTube, which earns her around $2.5 million.

Activity as a YouTuber as a Source of Income in Poland

The top Polish YouTubers earn much less than the global stars of YouTube. It is estimated that 1.5 million views of Polish videos translate into compensation of around $300—the rate for advertising viewed by Poles is thus more or less ten times less than in the case of Americans (Pająk, 2015). For this reason, the bulk of income for Polish YouTubers does not come from broadcasting advertisements, but from partnerships, advertising contracts, participation on television programs or work as brand ambassadors. Selected examples of this kind of activity by leading Polish YouTubers are discussed below.

Sylwester Wardęga, creator of the channel SA Wardega, is currently the Polish YouTuber who has earned the most in an international career. His video *Mutant Giant Spider Dog* was in first place in the list *2014's most-watched YouTube videos* published by the Independent Mail (Davis, n.d.)—in 2014 alone, the video was seen by 118.7 million viewers. YouTube awarded Wardęga the YouTube Rewind prize for the most popular video of 2014 ("Sylwester Wardęga wygrał", 2014). It should be noted, however, that Wardęga's channel has a much greater international potential than those of other Polish creators, because the intent is not to have spoken language at all. All of the videos are pranking videos, and Wardęga uses only sound and images. The pranking videos hosted on YouTube are similar in character to older media productions, particularly on television, which were designed to surprise or startle random people and record their reactions (Hobbs, 2011, p. 32). On the Internet, this is not entirely new either; the fashion for pranking videos has been ongoing since 2002, when the first of this kind of production began to appear, belonging to one of two types, so-called *scary pranks* (the joke relying on frightening people in public spaces) or *scary mazes* (in which a person is startled by an image appearing suddenly on a computer screen) (Hobbs & Grafe, 2015). With his productions, Wardęga skillfully participated in this trend. As a result of his huge popularity, in 2015 he was invited to sit on the panel of jurors of the program *Przygarnij mnie* ["Give me a home"], which has been broadcast on TVP2 of Polish Television since March 2015.

Radosław Kotarski, who is a qualified attorney, began with public lectures given in Krakow. When he published his first video, *Dama z gronostajem* [the Lady with an Ermine] on YouTube, however, it turned out it was able to attract hundreds of viewers online (Gąsior, 2013). In August 2012, the Polimaty channel was launched, which currently has 362,038 subscribers and a total number of 35,354,894 views.[2] In September 2014, Bank Millennium launched a national television campaign in Poland, for which a cycle of spots was made featuring Kotarski. What is more, the spots were made in such a way (type of narration, introduction and so on) as to follow as closely as possible the style used by Kotarski in his videos on his Polimaty channel.

Jacek Walkiewicz, a psychologist and personal development trainer, academic instructor and member of the Polish Professional Public Speakers Association [*Stowarzyszenie Profesjonalnych Mówców*], became a recognizable and popular figure when, on February 12, 2013, his 20-minute TEDx talk entitled *The Full Power of Possibility* [*Pełna moc możliwości*] was published (TEDx is an international series of public talks organized by the non-profit Sapling Foundation founded by Chris Anderson in 1996). Since then, the film has been seen by 1,595,337 viewers.[3] In June 2014, Walkiewicz was hired to take part in a national advertising campaign in Poland for ING ("Jacek Walkiewicz motywuje", 2014), including television, Internet, radio, outdoor advertising as well as in branches of ING Bank Śląski.

5 Sposobów na... is a channel that was launched on YouTube on July 3, 2013. Posted there are short lifehacking videos, in other words tips showing users simple tricks that make life easier. Lifehacking emerged from hacker culture, but its steady growth in popularity over the past few years in mass culture has caused the idea itself to undergo some changes. While innovativeness is still the key feature of lifehacking, the current priority is simplifying many areas of everyday life and giving advice in the simplest possible way (Pręgowski, 2007). This approach is taken by the creators of the channel *5 Sposobów na...*, which currently has 1,362,294 subscribers, generating a total of 180,486,909 views.[4] Each of the top ten most popular videos on this channel have received over 2 million views. In March, the creators of *5 Sposobów na...* began working in advertising and promotion with Castorama Polska, taking part in commercials broadcast on national television channels in Poland. The advertisement is based on exactly the same narrative features as the videos posted on *5 Sposobów na…*, and the cooperation resulted in surprisingly rapid effects: within only 45 days, Castorama's YouTube channel gained 85,000 new subscribers (Marszałek, 2015). After three months, Castorama surpassed the largest global chain of stores of its kind, Office Depot, in number of subscriptions (Marszałek, 2015).

Emil the Photo Radar Hunter [*Emil łowca fotoradarów*] is a series of YouTube videos on the TVBigos channel, launched by Emil Rau on June 29, 2006. The topics of the channel are automotive, chiefly the location of traffic enforcement cameras, commonly called photo radars that, according to the findings of the channel owner, are set up by local police officers in violation of Polish regulations. Currently, TVBigos has 39,233 subscribers and 16,406,259 views.[5] In 2013, the creators of TVBigos began to cooperate with the national thematic channel TVN Turbo, which has resulted in TVN Turbo broadcasting a cyclical program *Emil the Photo Radar Hunter*. Each season (currently the third is being broadcast) consists of ten 22-minute episodes.

Łukasz Jakóbiak is a key figure among those in Poland who communicate with audiences using YouTube—as the first to do so in Poland, he created an innovative format, known until then only on television, yet destined for the Internet. This format is a new type of talk show, on which celebrities are invited, but the conversation itself takes place without the participation of the public, and the set is the creator's studio apartment. This move is an excellent example of adaptation of what had formerly been a television format of interviews with well-known people to a new medium: YouTube (Barczyk, 2013, p. 268).

Following Jakóbiak's career, one can trace the interest from both brands and national television channels in the viewing statistics of his channel. Jakóbiak, himself a performer known from such undertakings as *Fernando* ("Jakóbiak zaprojektował kolekcję znanej marki", n.d.; "Madonna podobna do Matki Boskiej", 2009) or *Keep rocking Poland*, tried to find a position at television stations many times. Although he offered to host a program on which he would interview stars, there was no interest from any station. On April 19, 2012, he decided to start his own YouTube channel, on which he wanted to carry out his idea for television. The set for the program was a 20-square-meter studio apartment in Warsaw's Mokotow district, to which he has invited stars of the cinema, the stage, and the media since 2012.

Jakóbiak combines several traits that are very important from the perspective of personal branding. As Schawbel (2010) emphasizes, the talented today achieve success where "in the public sphere, a cluster of individuals are given greater presence and a wider scope of activity and agency than are those who make up the rest of the population. They are followed to move on the public stage while the rest of us watch" (p. ix).

Jakóbiak creates his own personal brand on the basis of the following key traits:

(a) being a journalist with a positive attitude who is interested in people
(b) being a fashionably dressed man who cares about his appearance
(c) being a person extremely well-versed in the world of celebrities and media.

In addition, he uses elements of storytelling: he introduces himself (truthfully) as an autograph hunter who comes from a small town, who now invites celebrities to his small apartment in Warsaw.

In the three years the channel 20m² has existed, Łukasz Jakóbiak has worked with many companies and brands, including Agora SA, the o2 web portal, Jameson Irish Whiskey, Bank Millennium, Warsaw Fashion Weekend 2012, Clip Clip, Bee Free, Google, Durex, Old Spice, Absolut, Kazadi, Polsat, T-Mobile, Jameson, Sony IFA, TVN Media News, PayU, Compensa, ING, Wedel, Heyah, Danone and Grants. In the same period Łukasz Jakóbiak became an ambassador for brands such as Sony (since July 2015) and Apple (since July 2013) ("Jakóbiak zaprojektował kolekcję znanej marki", n.d.).

The scale of interest on the part of brands in working with Jakóbiak and the time in which this took place shows the enormous marketing possibilities that arise from professionally creating a personal brand using YouTube. Aside from the marketing benefits in the form of participation in events, advertisements and product placement, proposals for work with national television channels have appeared. The first television effect of Jakóbiak's work on YouTube was his nomination for the Wiktor award, which has been awarded since 1985 by the Polish Television Academy, in the category of Television Discovery of 2012. ("Znamy nominacje do Wiktorów", 2013). That same year, he received the Best Dressed Man award from *Fashion Magazine* in the category of Best Dressed Man in Pop-culture ("Łukasz Jakóbiak: Najlepiej ubranym", 2012) and, in 2013, the Best Dressed Pole award from *Logo24* magazine in the category of Stylish Man of the Year

2013 (Swoboda, 2014). Also in 2013, Łukasz Jakóbiak made his debut on Polish national television. On June 9, 2013 he was the emcee for the TOPtrendy 2013 gala presentation during the annual TOPtrendy Music Festival in Sopot. In the final months of 2016, Łukasz Jakóbiak received proposals for hosting his own talk show on one of the largest national commercial television stations in Poland.[6]

Value of the Advertising Market on YouTube

Net revenues from advertising on YouTube on the American market alone in 2014 were $1.13 billion, which was 18.9% of the video advertising market in the United States. Net revenue from video advertisements includes only material that appears when a video is opened in a window, and does not include earnings from banners, search results or other advertisements on the service ("YouTube owns nearly 20%", 2014).

Even though the advertising market on YouTube is constantly growing, its potential is still not fully exploited, because the advertising is not consistent with the content that it precedes. At the same time, the diversity of channels and user profiles on YouTube mean that advertisements could be precisely tailored to their audiences ("YouTube owns nearly 20%", 2014).

The revenues from YouTube's largest partner networks are also substantial. According to a report by Ampere Analysis, these reach $21 million annually from advertisements and partnership agreements with brands ("7,4 mln dol. w rok", 2015).

Main Directions of Change in the Ways of Shaping a Personal Brand in the United States and in Poland

Online media and social media are becoming the basic sources of knowledge about brands and products for many consumers, and also play an important role in the creation of a personal brand. The real motor driving every brand today is user recommendations, which is why creating a loyal network of customers is so important—people who know the given brand well and are glad to take advantage of what it offers them.

Technological change also forces change in the area of designing a personal brand. Phenomena like the increasing popularity of video content, especially among younger people, members of Generations Y and Z, the development of Smart TV[7] or the wide availability and recognizability of

YouTube mean that currently it is difficult to create a personal brand without creating video content.

This is all the more so given that the service itself encourages young, non-professional creators of content and makes it possible for its most active users to record content in professional studios. A team created for this very purpose, YouTube Space, helps creators produce material, and offers strategy programs and workshops.

These take place in the YouTube Space production studies in Los Angeles, New York, London, Tokyo, São Paulo and Berlin. As of March 2015, over 10,000 videos were produced in YouTube Space studios, which altogether have received over 1 billion views and over 70 million viewer hours ("YouTube dla prasy", n.d.). YouTube Space can be used free of charge by anyone whose YouTube channel has at least 5000 subscribers (Saska, 2014).

NOTES

1. Based on data available on individual channels, as of August 9, 2015.
2. Data available at https://www.youtube.com/user/Polimaty, as of August 8, 2015.
3. Data available at https://www.youtube.com/watch?v=ktjMz7c3ke4, as of August 9, 2015.
4. Data available at https://www.youtube.com/user/5SposobowNa, as of August 9, 2015.
5. Data available at https://www.youtube.com/user/TVBigos, as of August 9, 2015.
6. Internal information obtained from the LifeTube agency, which represents Łukasz Jakóbiak.
7. In the first year after SmartTV became popular, the audience for this kind of solution already constituted a larger group than the clients of large cable operators. Cf. Wierzbowska (2014, p. 216).

REFERENCES

7,4 mln dol. w rok. Tyle na YouTube zarobił 25-letni Szwed. (2015, July 9). Retrieved from http://www.forbes.pl/pewdiepie-zarobil-na-youtube-1-4-mln-dol-w-rok,artykuly,196907,1,1.html

Barczyk, A. (2013). Internetowy talk-show – odmiana rodzajowa czy nowy gatunek? Charakterystyka programu 20 m2 Łukasza, *Acta Universitatis Lodziensis. Folia Litteraria Polonica, 2*(20), 255–270.

Berg, M. (2015, October 14). The world's highest-paid YouTube stars 2015. *Forbes.* Retrieved from http://www.forbes.com/sites/maddieberg/2015/10/14/the-worlds-highest-paid-youtube-stars-2015/#2197fde3542c

Bójko, M. (2014, April 8). *Smart TV: cwaniak z tego telewizora.* Retrieved from http://wyborcza.pl/1,75400,15759660,Smart_TV_cwaniak_z_tego_telewizora_PORADNIK_.html

Czterokrotny wzrost liczby użytkowników serwisu YouTube w osiem lat. (2015, February 12). Retrieved from https://www.gemius.pl/wydawcy-aktualnosci/czterokrotny-wzrost-liczby-uzytkownikow-youtubea-w-osiem-lat.html

Davis, C. (n.d.). *2014's most popular music, movies and web videos.* Retrieved from http://www.independentmail.com/news/national/2014s-most-popular-music-movies-and-web-videos

Do you have any favorite YouTube channels that you watch regularly?. (n.d.). Retrieved from http://www.statista.com/statistics/259490/us-users-who-regularly-watch-favourite-youtube-channels

Domaradzki, K. (2015, October 15). *Najlepiej zarabiający youtuberzy 2015.* Retrieved from http://www.forbes.pl/youtube-2015-ranking-najlepiej-zarabiajacych-youtuberow,artykuly,199726,1,1.html

Duda, T. (2016, March 2). *10 najlepszych smartfonów do zdjęć i filmów.* Retrieved from http://www.benchmark.pl/testy_i_recenzje/najlepsze-smartfony-do-zdjec-i-filmow.html

El Rubius. (n.d.). *Wikipedia.* Retrieved April 11, 2016, from https://en.wikipedia.org/wiki/El_Rubius

Filmy w technologii 360° na YouTube! Jak to działa?. (2015, June 26). Retrieved from http://www.brief.pl/artykul,3003,filmy_w_technologii_360_na_youtube_jak_to_dziala.html

Gąsior, M. (2013, July 13). Radek Kotarski, twórca programu 'Polimaty': Jestem jednoosobową redakcją naukową. *YouTube to przyszłość.* Retrieved from http://natemat.pl/68089,radek-kotarski-tworca-programu-polimaty-jestem-jednoosobowa-redakcja-naukowa-telewizja-jest-przestarzala-youtube-to-przyszlosc

Germán Garmendia. (n.d.). *Wikipedia.* Retrieved April 11, 2015, from https://en.wikipedia.org/wiki/Germán_Garmendia

Gross, D. (2014, December 9). *YouTube's most popular video of 2014 was....* Retrieved from http://edition.cnn.com/2014/12/09/tech/web/top-youtube-videos-2014

Gwóźdź, M. (2014, May 13). *Internet w codziennym życiu – raport Google.* Retrieved from http://smmeasure.eu/internet-codziennym-zyciu-raport-google

High-tech. (n.d.). *Cambridge advanced learner's dictionary & thesaurus.* Retrieved from http://dictionary.cambridge.org/dictionary/english/high-tech

Hobbs, R. (2011). *Digital and media literacy: The pleasures and perils of online pranking.* ASCA School Counselor. Retrieved from http://mediaeducationlab.

com/sites/default/files/Hobbs%2520School%2520Counselor%2520Nov%
25202011_0.pdf

Hobbs, R., & Grafe, S. (2015). YouTube ranking cross cultures. *First Monday, 20*,
7. Retireved from http://www.firstmonday.dk/ojs/index.php/fm/article/vie
w/5981/4699

Jacek Walkiewicz motywuje w reklamach ING Banku Śląskiego. (2014, May 26).
Retrieved from http://www.wirtualnemedia.pl/artykul/jacek-walkiewicz-mo
tywuje-w-reklamach-ing-banku-slaskiego-wideo

Jakóbiak zaprojektował kolekcję znanej marki. (n.d.). Retrieved from http://www.
fakt.pl/styl/lukasz-jakobiak-zaprojektowal-kolekcje-znanej-marki,artykul
y,512912.html

Jenna Marbles. (n.d.). *Wikipedia.* Retrieved April 11, 2016, from https://en.wiki
pedia.org/wiki/Jenna_Marbles

Kamiński, P. (2013, March 8). *Streaming – oglądanie zamiast grania czy zaczątek
telewizji dla graczy?* Retrieved from http://polygamia.pl/streaming-ogladanie-
zamiast-grania-czy-zaczatek-telewizji-dla-graczy

Kowalski, P. (2013, August 2). *Czym jest płatność online? Szybkie i wygodne płatności
w internecie.* Retrieved from http://www.money.pl/eurobank/zdaniem-ekspe
rta/konta-i-bankowosc-elektroniczna/artykul/czym;jest;platnosc;online;
szybkie;i;wygodne;platnosci;w;internecie,243,0,1355763.html

Leniwiec. (2013, December 22). *Test: którą kamerę GoPro wybrać? Porównanie
modeli Hero 3 White, Hero 3 Black i Hero 3+ Black.* Retrieved from http://an
tymoto.com/test-ktora-kamere-gopro-wybrac-porownanie-modeli-hero-3-white-
hero-3-black-hero-3-black

List of the most subscribed users on YouTube. (n.d.). *Wikipedia.* Retrieved April
11, 2016, from https://en.wikipedia.org/wiki/List_of_the_most_subscribed
_users_on_YouTube

Łukasz Jakóbiak: Najlepiej ubranym mężczyzną według Fashion Magazine! (2012,
October 24). Retrieved from http://gwiazdy.wp.pl/artykul
/5856503007532161/lukasz-jakobiak-najlepiej-ubranym-mezczyzna-wedlug-fa
shion-magazine.html

Madonna podobna do Matki Boskiej zawisła na moście. (2009, August 13).
Retrieved from http://wiadomosci.wp.pl/kat,1345,title,Madonna-podobna-
do-Matki-Boskiej-zawisla-na-moscie,wid,11398323,wiadomosc.html?ticaid
=11566d

Marszałek, P. (2015, April 9). *Współpraca Castoramy i "5 sposobów na" to wzór do
naśladowania dla innych marek.* Retrieved from http://natemat.pl/139047,wspol
praca-castoramy-i-5-sposobow-na-to-wzor-do-nasladowania-dla-innych-marek

Miotk, A. (2014, May 16). *Jak Polacy korzystają z serwisu YouTube – garść danych.*
Retrieved from http://annamiotk.pl/jak-polacy-korzystaja-z-youtube-garsc-
danych/

Najlepiej zarabiający youtuberzy na świecie. (2015, October 18). Retrieved from http://www.radiozet.pl/Rozrywka/O-tym-sie-mowi/Najbogatsi-youtuberzy-na-swiecie-RANKING-00012948

Niemycki, A. (2011, June 6). *Który aparat jest najlepszy do kręcenia filmów?* Retrieved from http://www.chip.pl/artykuly/foto-wi-deo/2011/06/ktory-aparat-jest-najlepszy-do-filmow

Pająk, P. (2015, January 19). *Krzysztof Gonciarz szczerze o zarabianiu na YouTube i porównaniu do zarobków blogerów.* Retrieved from http://www.spidersweb.pl/2015/01/krzysztof-gonciarz-zarabianiu-youtube.html

Percentage of U.S. internet users who have a YouTube account as of March 2013. (2013, March). Retrieved from http://www.statista.com/statistics/256895/share-of-us-internet-users-who-have-a-youtube-account

Pieczonka, K. (2013, January 27). *Japończycy przyśpieszają telewizję 4K, start w lipcu 2014.* Retrieved from http://www.frazpc.pl/aktualnosci/923520,japonczycy-przyspieszaja-telewizje-4k-start-w-lipcu-2014.html

Pisarski, M. (2015, August 21). *Test Samsung Gear VR dla Galaxy S6: Wirtualna rzeczywistość od Samsunga.* Retrieved from http://www.komputerswiat.pl/testy/sprzet/urzadzenia-multimedialne/2015/08/samsung-gear-vr-dla-gala xy-s6-test.aspx

Poczęsna, J. (2014, January 3). *Personal branding – czyli jak zbudować markę osobistą w sieci?* Retrieved from http://www.bankier.pl/wiadomosc/Personal-branding-czyli-jak-zbudowac-marke-osobista-w-sieci-3027890.html

Połowianiuk, M. (2014, November 28). *"Kijek selfie" jest nielegalny. I bardzo dobrze!* Retrieved from http://www.spider-sweb.pl/2014/11/kijek-selfie.html

Poznaj najpopularniejsze produkty elektroniczne marca: ranking. (2016, March 6). Retrieved from http://www.komputerswiat.pl/artykuly/redakcyjne/2016/04/poznaj-najpopularniejsze-produkty-elektroniczne-marca-ranking,3.aspx

Pręgowski, M. P. (2007). Lifehacking: A new social phenomenon inspired by hacker culture. *Studia Medioznawcze, 3*(30). Retrieved from http://studiamedioznawcze.pl/Numery/2007_3_30/pregowski-en.pdf

Ryan Higa. (n.d.). *Wikipedia.* Retrieved April 11, 2016, from https://en.wikipedia.org/wiki/Ryan_Higa

Saska, M. (2014, November 5). *YouTube Space: przestrzeń niewirtualna.* Retrieved from http://alfabloger.pl/youtube-space-przestrzen-niewirtualna

Schawbel, D. (2010). *Me 2.0, 4 steps to building your future.* New York: Kaplan Publishing.

Seitz, P. (2015, August 7). *Action camera market to see growth through 2019.* Retrieved from http://www.inves-tors.com/news/technology/gopro-to-benefit-from-action-camera-market-growth-futuresource

Sippey, M. (2013, January 24). *Vine: A new way to share video.* Retrieved from https://blog.twitter.com/2013/vine-a-new-way-to-share-video

Smart TV alliance – LG i Philips ze wspólnym standardem dla aplikacji. (2012, June 25). Retrieved from http://www.wirtualnemedia.pl/artykul/smart-tv-alliance-lg-i-philips-ze-wspolnym-standardem-dla-aplikacji

Snapchat's audience is teen-y. Usage of the disappearing photo-sharing app is still low in the US. (2014, October 21). Retrieved from http://www.emarketer.com/Article.aspx?R=1011335

Statistics and facts about YouTube. (n.d.). Retrieved from http://www.statista.com/topics/2019/youtube

Swoboda, A. (2014, January 23). *Wybraliście najlepiej ubranego Polaka 2013 roku.* Retrieved from http://www.logo24.pl/Logo24/56,85825,15318687,Wybrali scie_najlepiej_ubranego_Polaka_2013_roku.html

Sylwester Wardęga wygrał YouTube Rewind. (2014, December 10). *Spodziewałem się 30, ale nie 100 milionów odsłon.* Retrieved from http://www.wirtualnemedia.pl/artykul/sylwester-wardega-wygral-youtube-rewind-spodziewalem-sie-30-ale-nie-100-milionow-odslon

Szewczyk, Ł. (2015, June 13). *Megapanel kwiecień 2015: YouTube i główne portale tracą użytkowników, zyskuje Facebook.* Retrieved from http://media2.pl/badania/123955-Megapanel-kwiecien-2015-You-Tube-i-glowne-portale-traca-uzytko wnikow-zyskuje-Facebook.html

Szewczyk, O. (2015, January 13). *Najważniejszym wynalazkiem 2014 roku okazał się... kijek.* Retrieved from http://wyborcza.pl/1,75400,17246397,Najwazniej szym_wynalazkiem_2014_roku_okazal_sie_.html

Ułan, G. (2015, March 13). *YouTube wkracza w nowy wymiar, czyli filmy 360 stopni.* Retrieved from http://antyweb.pl/youtube-wkracza-w-nowy-wymiar-czyli-film y-360-stopni

VanossGaming. (n.d.). *Wikipedia.* Retrieved April 11, 2016, from https://en.wiki pedia.org/wiki/VanossGaming

Wierzbowska, T. (2014). Wideo i audio w sieci. In J. Królewski & P. Sala (Eds.), *E-marketing* (pp. 213–230). Warsaw, Poland: Wydawnictwo Naukowe PWN.

YouTube dla prasy. (n.d.). Retrieved from https://www.youtube.com/yt/press/pl/statistics.html

YouTube owns nearly 20% share of US digital video ads. Google's network is feeling heat from AOL, Yahoo, others. (2014, September 11). Retrieved from http://www.emarketer.com/Article/YouTube-Owns-Nearly-20-Share-of-US-Digital-Video-Ads/1011191#sthash.YcPRJKMq.dpuf

YouTube spotlight. (n.d.). *Wikipedia.* Retrieved April 11, 2016, from https://en.wikipedia.org/wiki/YouTube_Spotlight

YouTube Trends 06.2015. (2015, June). Retrieved from http://www.sotrender.pl/trends/youtube/reports/201506/categories

Youtube.com. (n.d.-a). Retrieved from https://www.youtube.com/user/5Spo sobowNa

Youtube.com. (n.d.-b). Retrieved from https://www.youtube.com/user/Polimaty

Youtube.com. (n.d.-c). Retrieved from https://www.youtube.com/user/TVBigos

Youtube.com. (n.d.-d). Retrieved from https://www.youtube.com/watch?v=ktj Mz7c3ke4

Znamy nominacje do Wiktorów 2012. (2013, April 2). Retrieved from http://www.tvp.pl/rozrywka/aktualnosci/znamy-nominacje-do-wiktorow-2012/105 99797

Zyskują coraz większą popularność. Zobacz, gdzie drony wkrótce mogą być wykorzystane. (2016, January 3). Retrieved from http://www.money.pl/gospodarka/wiadomosci/artykul/zyskuja-coraz-wieksza-popularnosc-zobacz-,133,0,1988229.html

Personal Branding Using YouTube in the United States and in Poland, as Shown by the Results of Empirical Research

Abstract The author's own empirical research is discussed in this chapter. The methodological assumptions of the research are characterized, including the research questions, goals and hypotheses, and the characteristics of the study group are given. The results of this research are presented in two parts: a qualitative one, based on case studies of recognized YouTubers in Poland, and a quantitative one, based on a questionnaire given to two groups of respondents (young Internet users in Poland and in the United States).

Keywords Empirical research • Qualitative research • Quantitative research • YouTubers • Case studies

GOALS AND METHODOLOGICAL FOUNDATIONS OF THE RESEARCH

The primary goal of this work is to identify and compare strategies for shaping a personal brand among young Polish and American internauts and YouTubers who are examples of personal branding success, and to identify a set of effective practices in this area.

The following hypotheses are formulated in this work:

Primary hypothesis: YouTube is one of the most effective tools for shaping a personal brand for members of the young generation (Generations Y and Z).

© The Author(s) 2018
M. Grzesiak, *Personal Brand Creation in the Digital Age*,
https://doi.org/10.1007/978-3-319-69697-3_5

Secondary hypothesis: Professional preparation of a personal brand on YouTube is becoming a passport to gaining a presence in traditional media and to receiving advertising contracts.

In order to verify the above hypotheses, an empirical study was designed. The research consisted of two parts—qualitative and quantitative. The general design of the research is presented in Fig. 5.1.

The primary research goals in the qualitative part were initial exploration of the topic, enriching understanding of the researched topic and detailed analysis of the phenomenon through case studies. The author of this work is well aware of the primacy of quantitative methods in contemporary management science (Burnewicz, 2007; Czakon, 2009, pp. 13–18), but in order to investigate this relatively new topic of creating a personal brand by young people, it is necessary to go beyond the methodological limits of quantitative research.

The primary goal of the quantitative part was to gather data that would allow confirmation or rejection of the research hypotheses. The specific research goals include above all:

(a) to determine whether the respondents know the concept of a "personal brand" and what their associations with the term are
(b) to verify whether the researched subjects build their own personal brand
(c) to investigate for what purpose and by use of which social media do those studied build a personal brand
(d) to investigate what—according to the respondents—the strong and weak sides of the YouTube service are as a medium for building a personal brand
(e) to verify which tools (which specific social media) the respondents use to achieve selected goals linked with building a personal brand
(f) to investigate their perception of activity on YouTube as a source of revenue
(g) to determine whether the respondents recognize social media stars and, if they are interested in them, which social media they use to receive the content the stars publish.

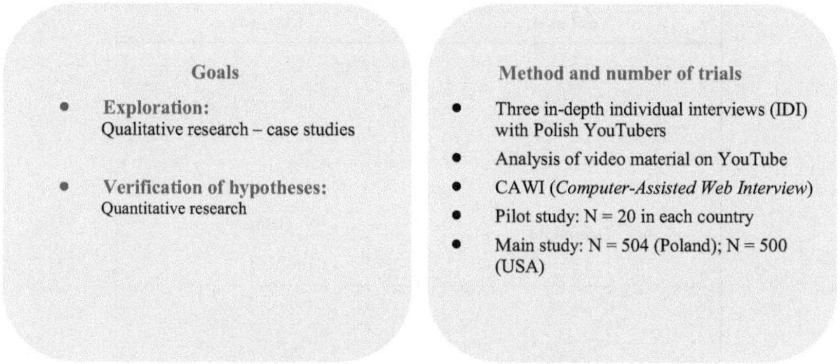

Goals	Method and number of trials
• Exploration: Qualitative research – case studies	• Three in-depth individual interviews (IDI) with Polish YouTubers • Analysis of video material on YouTube
• Verification of hypotheses: Quantitative research	• CAWI (*Computer-Assisted Web Interview*) • Pilot study: N = 20 in each country • Main study: N = 504 (Poland); N = 500 (USA)

Fig. 5.1   General design of the study (Source: Own elaboration)

Methodology of the Qualitative Research

The qualitative research consisted of analysis of case studies, which used the following methods:

1. Partially structured, in-depth interviews lasting ca. 1–1.5 hours. This method allowed enriched understanding of the research topic, simultaneously drawing on the individual experience of the respondent.
2. Analysis of video material from YouTube (material created by the interviewed YouTubers).

Number of interviews: 3

Dates research was conducted: January–March 2016

Sample selection: Targeted selection was used to ensure that the sample would consist of YouTubers addressing various topics: games, beauty and lifestyle. Participation was voluntary and, given the nature of the research, it was not anonymous (Fig. 5.2).

During the interviews, the following topics were raised with each person:

(a) perception of their own personal brand
(b) strategic goals of personal branding
(c) the practice of shaping a personal brand—methods and tools
(d) changes in their image over the time they have been on YouTube
(e) ways of measuring their own image

YouTuber	Category
Red Lipstick Monster	Beauty
Jaś Dąbrowski	Games
Wapniak	Lifestyle

Fig. 5.2 Information regarding the qualitative research sample (case studies) (Source: Own elaboration)

- (f) benchmarks and models
- (g) factors affecting success and failure
- (h) plans for the future.

Methodology of the Quantitative Research

The research for this work was conducted using the method of an online questionnaire (CAWI—Computer-Assisted Web Interview). The questionnaire was programmed using Qualtrics software. The respondents were participants in a commercial online consumer panel by Research Now, an international market research company.

The questionnaire consisted mainly of closed questions, including questions using a scale (primarily a five-point Likert scale), cafeteria-style disjunctive and conjunctive questions as well as alternatives.

The questionnaire also included a few open questions in which respondents had the opportunity to make statements more freely and in greater depth.

It was assumed for the research that because of globalization, the spread of the Internet and the free access to social media, the mechanisms for creating a personal brand operate in a universal manner (regardless of the country of residence). In terms of location, the research was conducted in

Poland and in the United States. It was conducted online, bearing the following premises in mind:

(a) The research topic of creating a personal brand using social media requires access to respondents who use the Internet.
(b) Young people, both in Poland and the United States, mostly use the Internet. In Poland, 97% of people aged 18–24 use the Internet, and 95% of those aged 25–34 use it. In the United States, the percentage of people aged 18–34 who use the Internet is 96%. One can thus assume that the opinions of Internet users of these groups reflect the views of the majority of the population of this age range.
(c) Research practice has shown that research conducted via the Internet has become a fully fledged research method and is constantly gaining in popularity.

The research, conducted on two groups of people, is comparative in nature. How to conduct international comparative research has been the subject of a rich body of literature, discussion of which is beyond the scope of this work. However, the author was well aware of the many rigorous demands that international research must meet (such as, for example, the equivalence of research subjects, of measurement, of research samples as well as the equivalence of direct research procedures) (Szarucki, 2010, pp. 51–66).

The research sample in both countries consisted of members of the young generation (aged 18–34) who regularly use the Internet and social media. The questionnaire was identical in both countries (except for a few questions of a demographic nature, for example, questions about racial identification in the questionnaire for residents of the United States). The questionnaire was verified in terms of merit and language by an American market researcher who is also an editor of texts in the social sciences. Code keys to the open questions were also verified by an American market researcher, as was the coding of the open questions. The research was conducted on both groups simultaneously.

Time needed for completion of the questionnaire: ca. 15 min.
Date research was conducted: May 2016
Statistical analyses: Statistica 10.0 software (StatSoft Inc., 2011) was used for statistical analysis. For verification of statistical hypotheses, the chi-squared test was used. The level of significance was set at

$\alpha = 0.05$. The null hypothesis was rejected when the p-value was calculated at $p < 0.05$.

Above all, the differences in the results received from respondents in Poland and the United States were analyzed on the whole sample.

In addition, the following specific analyses were conducted:

(a) within a given country (for example, the difference between women and men in Poland and between women and men in the United States); after initial analysis of the data, further analysis considered gender, age, education and size of the place of residence
(b) comparison of the results between countries within the subgroups of age and gender (for example, women in Poland compared with women in the United States).

Results of the comparative analysis of Poland and the United States were shown for each case in which they were conducted. Because of the limited scope of this work, the results of the analysis on subgroups were shown only when the author felt that they contributed something new and showed the topic in an interesting way.

Contingency tables were prepared with the data and analysis module of Qualtrics software.

DESCRIPTION OF THE RESPONDENTS

Sample size: 1004 respondents aged 18–34, of whom 504 were from Poland and 500 from the United States.

Sampling technique: quota sampling.

Description of respondents: The research was conducted on a sample of Polish and American subjects, assuming such quotas as to ensure that the demographic structure of the samples would reflect, as accurately as possible, the structure of the population of young consumers (18–34 years of age) in both countries in regard to age, gender and place of residence.

Quotas were developed on the basis of data from the following sources:

1. **Poland:** Central Statistical Office of Poland (2016, n.d.)
2. **United States:**

(a) United States Census Bureau (n.d.)
(b) The Urban Land Institute, which published the results of research it conducted on a representative sample of millennials in a report entitled *Gen Y and Housing* (2015)
(c) Bureau of Labor Statistics (n.d.).

Other conditions that had to be met for participation in the research were:

(a) familiarity with at least three social media platforms, one of which had to be YouTube
(b) use of YouTube at least three times a week.

The above conditions were dictated by the assumption that it is precisely people who actively use social media that will be the best source of insight into how young people shape a personal brand and what tools they use. Because this work regards the shaping of a personal brand using YouTube, it was important that respondents were active users of this service.

The author is of course aware that a sample constructed in this manner is not fully representative of the population of both countries, but to gain such a fully representative sample for the millennial generation would be quite difficult and expensive. In the United States, the research was conducted in English, which means that it was much easier to reach people whose first language is English, which currently is about 75% of young people (United States Census Bureau, 2014).

Those who do not use YouTube were excluded, but this was done intentionally. Use of a fully representative sample might also result in the information obtained on the topic of personal branding not being as in-depth as that obtained from the sample constructed for this research.

The most important parameters describing the research sample are presented in Tables 5.1, 5.2, 5.3, 5.4, and 5.5, below.

In the case of Polish voivodships, the sample selected reflected as accurately as possible the structure of the population. When it comes to size of the place of residence, there was an over-representation of people living in larger cities and towns (over 20,000 residents): in the sample 69% of respondents lived in such places, whereas 47% of young Poles live in cities and towns of that size. Village residents and smaller towns thus are underrepresented (31% of the research group vs. 53% of young Poles). This results from the enrolment requirements for the study (frequency of use of YouTube). It was decided, however, to continue with this sample to maintain the ability to compare the results between Poland and the United States.

Table 5.1 Age of respondents (%)

	Poland (N = 504) (%)	USA (N = 500) (%)
18–24	35	41
25–29	30	30
30–34	35	29

Source: Own research

Table 5.2 Gender of respondents (%)

	Poland (N = 504) (%)	USA (N = 500) (%)
Women	49	50
Men	51	50

Source: Own research

Table 5.3 Place of residence—voivodship[a], Poland (%)

	Poland (N = 504) (%)
Dolnośląskie[b]	8
Kujawsko-pomorskie	6
Lubelskie	6
Lubuskie	2
Łódzkie	6
Małopolskie	9
Mazowieckie	15
Opolskie	3
Podkarpackie	5
Podlaskie	3
Pomorskie	5
Śląskie	12
Świętokrzyskie	3
Warmińsko-mazurskie	3
Wielkopolskie	10
Zachodniopomorskie	4

Source: Own research
[a] For further reference about the administrative subdivision of Poland please check: https://en.wikipedia.org/wiki/Voivodeships_of_Poland
[b] Translator's note: For the convenience of readers who are interested in a further research but may not be familiar with Polish and the administrative subdivision of Poland, the translator decided to leave the original names of Polish voivodeships to make easier any reference to maps of Poland.

In the case of the type of location in the United States, there was a certain over-representation of people living in the center of cities or near them. This did not change the fundamental structure of the sample in regard to small-town, suburban and city residents.

Table 5.4 Size of place of residence, Poland (%)

	Poland (%)
Village	18
Town of up to 20,000 residents	13
City of 20,000–100,000 residents	23
City of 100,000–500,000 residents	25
City of over 500,000 residents	21

Source: Own research

Table 5.5 Region of residence, USA (%)

Regions	States included in the region	USA (N = 500) (%)
Region 1: Northeast	Maine, New Hampshire, Vermont, Massachusetts, Connecticut, Rhode Island, New Jersey, New York, Pennsylvania	18
Region 2: Midwest	North Dakota, South Dakota, Nebraska, Kansas, Missouri, Iowa, Minnesota, Wisconsin, Illinois, Michigan, Indiana, Ohio	21
Region 3: South	Maryland, Delaware, West Virginia, Virginia, Kentucky, Tennessee, North Carolina, South Carolina, Georgia, Florida, Alabama, Mississippi, Arkansas, Louisiana, Oklahoma, Texas, District of Columbia	37
Region 4: West	Washington, Idaho, Montana, Wyoming, Oregon, California, Nevada, Utah, Colorado, Arizona, New Mexico, Alaska, Hawaii	24

Source: Own research

Quotas were not imposed on the remaining traits, with the exception of the maximum number of unemployed persons allowed: here the number was set in accordance with the data on unemployment for the given age group. For the entire sample (18–34 years of age) this figure is 12% in Poland (Central Statistical Office of Poland, n.d.) and 7% in the United States (Bureau of Labor Statistics, n.d). The author proceeded from the assumption that the potential over-representation of unemployed persons in the sample could have an influence on the research results. The question of knowledge of the topic of personal branding or building one may be associated with how a respondent operates in the labor market. It turned out, however, that the percentage of unemployed persons in the research sample was lower than in the general population (which may result both from the low participation of unemployed persons in the research panels and from the low level of interest in personal branding among this group) (Table 5.6).

Table 5.6   Current professional status (%)

	Poland (N = 504) (%)	USA (N = 500) (%)
Student	26	28
Work full-time	58	60
Work part-time	11	16
Own a business	6	2
Maternity leave/homemaker	7	5
Unemployed	4	4
Other situation	2	0

Source: Own research
The percentages above do not add up to 100% because the respondents were allowed to choose several answers, as more than one option might describe their situation (for example, they could be students working part-time)

Table 5.7   Education, Poland (%)

	Poland (N = 504) (%)
Elementary school [*Podstawowe*]	1
Middle school [*Gimnazjalne*]	2
Trade school [*Zasadnicze zawodowe*]	4
High school [*Średnie*]	33
Undergraduate degree [*Studia licencjackie, inżynierskie, magisterskie*]	55
Postgraduate degree [*Studia podyplomowe, doktoranckie, MBA*]	5

Source: Own research

It turned out that the sample structure in terms of professional situation is similar in both countries, which has a favorable effect on comparability of the results.

Presented in Tables 5.10 and 5.11 below is information regarding the level of education achieved by the respondents. Given the different education systems, these results cannot be directly compared. However, in both countries around 60% of respondents had more than a secondary education (Tables 5.7 and 5.8).

The information presented in Tables 5.9, 5.10, and 5.11 regards household income as well as the self-perception of household financial situations. In Poland, the question is typically asked in terms of net monthly income,

Table 5.8 Education, USA (%)

	USA (N = 500) (%)
Less than high school	1
High school	23
Technical/vocational school	4
Associate's degree	14
Bachelor's degree	40
Post-graduate/professional degree	18

Source: Own research

Table 5.9 Monthly respondent net household income, Poland (%)

	Poland (N = 504) (%)
No income	2
Up to PLN 1000	4
PLN 1001–2000	13
PLN 2001–3000	14
PLN 3001–5000	29
PLN 5001–8000	19
Over PLN 8000	7
Don't know/hard to say	4
Prefer not to answer	8

Source: Own research

whereas in the United States this is typically a question of annual income before taxes. Much like in the case of education, these results cannot be directly compared. It is worth having a look at the answers to the question regarding how respondents evaluated their own material situation (Table 5.11). Less than 10% of respondents in either country see this as poor, and 60% of Poles and 48% of Americans as good. The remainder believe it to be average. Although there are clearly real differences visible both in income and in the evaluation of their household finances, the majority of those studied in each country rated their material situation as average or good.

Table 5.12 provides information about the race of the respondent (because Poland is essentially an ethnically homogeneous country, this question was only included in the questionnaire for residents of the United States).

Figures 5.3 and 5.4 show the prompted awareness of and use of social media in each country. An enrolment requirement was awareness of at least

Table 5.10 Respondent household total annual gross income, USA (%)

	USA (N = 500) (%)
No income	1
Under $25,000	13
$25,000–49,999	22
$50,000–74,999	23
$75,000–99,999	14
$100,000–149,999	13
Over $150,000	5
Don't know/hard to say	2
Prefer not to answer	7

Source: Own research

Table 5.11 Self-evaluation of household financial situation (%)

	Poland (N = 504) (%)	USA (N = 500) (%)
Very poor	1	1
Rather poor	5	6
Average	34	42
Rather good	48	31
Very good	12	17
Prefer not to answer	0	3

Source: Own research

Table 5.12 Respondent race, USA (%)

	USA (N = 500) (%)
White/Caucasian	62
African American	10
Hispanic	11
Asian	12
Other	2
Prefer not to say	3

Source: Own research

three social media platforms (of which YouTube had to be one), and it turned out that this criterion was met by nearly everyone interested in the research. Respondents were shown the name and logotype of each social media platform and asked about their awareness and use of it.

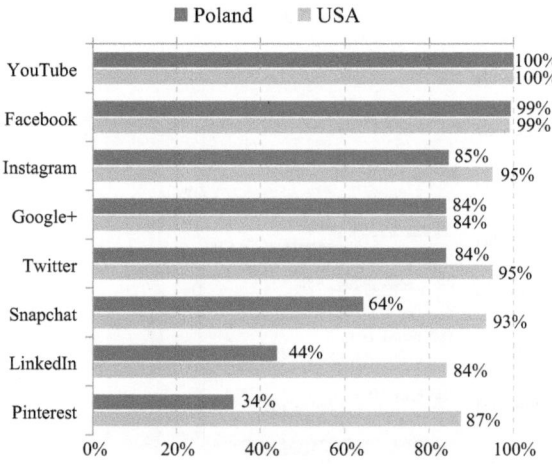

Fig. 5.3 Prompted awareness of social media ($N = 504$ (Poland); $N = 500$ (USA), entire sample. Source: Own research)

As can be seen in Figs. 5.3 and 5.4, awareness of YouTube, Facebook and Google+ is quite similar in both countries. Instagram and Twitter are a bit better known in the United States. There is great difference in favor of the United States in the case of awareness of Snapchat, LinkedIn and Pinterest.

Active use of YouTube was an enrolment requirement, and thus in each country 100% of respondents used this service. It turned out that if young people use YouTube, they do so frequently, even several times a day. The majority of people used the service every day or nearly every day (36% of respondents in Poland and 37% in the United States), and even several times a day (50% of respondents in Poland, and 43% in the United States, as illustrated in Table 5.13.

Among the remaining social media considered in the research, Facebook is used by a similar percentage of users in both groups (slightly higher in Poland). Polish respondents use Google+ decidedly more often than respondents from the United States, and all remaining social media are used more frequently by people researched residing in the United States.

Figure 5.5, which illustrates the character of the sample more clearly, regards activities that young people engage in on the Internet. As can be seen, respondents in Poland and the United States use the net in similar

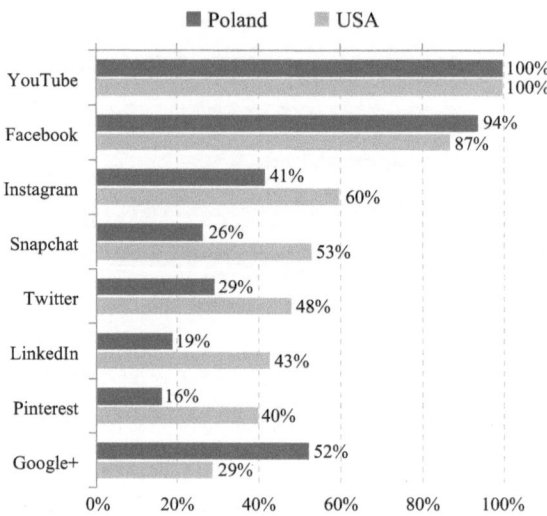

Fig. 5.4   Use of social media ($N = 504$ (Poland); $N = 500$ (USA), entire sample. Source: Own research)

Table 5.13   Frequency of use of YouTube (%)

	Poland (N = 504) (%)	USA (N = 500) (%)
Several times a day	50	43
Every day or almost every day	36	37
3–4 times a week	14	20

Source: Own research

ways. Of course, there are certain differences (for example, Poles read news or discuss and make comments, whereas Americans somewhat more often watch films and video clips), but the user profiles are similar. This corresponds to the author's expectations that result from many studies on globalization, especially in the case of the younger generation. This also has a positive effect on the comparability of the results between the countries.

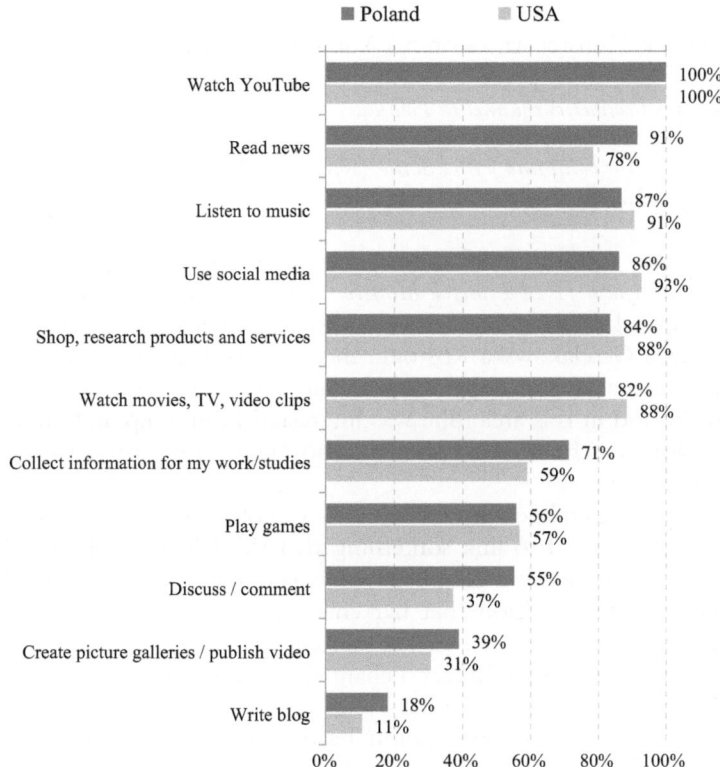

Fig. 5.5   Ways of using the Internet ($N = 504$ (Poland); $N = 500$ (USA), entire sample. Source: Own research)

RESEARCH RESULTS: QUALITATIVE PART (CASE STUDIES)

The primary goal of the interviews was to obtain information that would serve to identify the strategy for shaping a personal brand by the selected YouTubers. Each interview lasted ca. 1 hour and 15 minutes. An outline of the interview is included in Appendix 1.

Case Study: Red Lipstick Monster

Case Study: Red Lipstick Monster (Ewa Grzelakowska-Kostoglu, age 30). **Interview date:** February 22, 2016

History of the YouTuber
Red Lipstick Monster writes on her YouTube channel:

> *The biggest cosmetics channel in Poland.*
> *Different. More interesting.*
> *For real, to the point and with a smile.* (Red Lipstick Monster [Grzelakowska-Kostoglu, E.] 2015a)[1]

She is also the author of the makeup handbook *Red Lipstick Monster. Tajniki makijażu [Red Lipstick Monster. The Secrets of Makeup]* (2015b).

Red Lipstick Monster's presence on YouTube began on June 12, 2012. Earlier, Ewa Grzelakowska-Kostoglu thought about such a venture as she watched videos on YouTube about beauty and visage. She noticed huge gaps in Poland in this area. She was interested in makeup and knew how simple various techniques are, but that no one in Poland was showing or explaining them.

She did not then know how to create a videoblog from a technical point of view. She wanted to link something that she felt good about (visage, makeup) with something completely new (presence on YouTube, vlogs). She did not then envision that her channel would develop so well that would earn money from it. As she herself says, that was not a result of modesty, but because in 2012 no channel on YouTube was a commercial success.

Today, she is the leading Polish beauty vlogger. She recognizes the publishing of her book, *Red Lipstick Monster. Tajniki makijażu* (2015b) as her greatest success. This book became a bestseller in 2015 and opened the way to interesting business and media contacts for the author.

Red Lipstick Monster feels fulfilled and happy:

> *Without a doubt. Doing what I do, I feel I can reach what I set out to, I plan and direct my actions. I always dreamed about the kind of work where I would create something different from others. Independence, autonomy. I don't sit and think about and analyze things. I've got intuition. I feel good about that.*

She does say, however, that if she had known that her work on YouTube would develop as it did, she does not know whether she would have started it. It turns out that it has led to a kind of popularity that is a burden at times. In business, she cooperates with LifeTube (the largest multi-channel YouTube network in Poland).

The YouTuber's Perspective on Personal Branding: Associations,
Understanding, Relevance
A personal brand, in Red Lipstick Monster's opinion, is "*creating one's own*
slice of the world, work that you can somehow clearly name and describe. A
concrete creation that you can describe."

Her own personal brand is very important to Red Lipstick Monster. The
YouTuber is satisfied with her brand. She says that she is glad that "*there*
isn't a staff of people behind me. No analysis, just intuitively it works out so well
for me, and some others can't do that despite having a whole staff."

Perception of Her Own Personal Brand
The YouTuber sees herself, above all, as an open person, warm and helpful,
as an expert in the area of makeup. She helps people gain new abilities in
using makeup and makes selecting of products easier.

She possesses inner strength and motivation. She is consistent, coura-
geous and independent. She also has a very positive attitude toward life. She
is aware of being a highly distinctive and expressive person, mainly because
of her external appearance (hairstyle, tattoos and earrings).

The Practice of Shaping Her Personal Brand: Methods and Tools
Red Lipstick Monster is authentic and shows her true face: "*The traits that*
are in the image are an integral part of my person and I can't separate them
out. They just are."

Taught by experience, she excludes negative aspects of life. She says that
when someone is successful, they are met with a lack of understanding if
they speak of problems: "*You can't say that you're the same person.*"

The tutorials that she makes are high quality. In an accessible and
concrete way, she explains the process of applying a given kind of makeup.
The YouTuber applies it herself and shows the effects before and after. She
uses cosmetics from various brands and in different price categories.

She tries to show something more than just beauty tips. "*I manage to*
smuggle in some inner values: strength, motivation, action."

It should be mentioned that Red Lipstick Monster does more than the
typical tutorial videos. For example, a very interesting initiative was her film
The history of makeup in the 20th century [*Historia makiażu XX wieku*]
(posted in November 2015; by June 2016 it had over 900,000 views). She is
also increasing her entries into the lifestyle category as well.

For her, what is important is development, taking up new challenges.

She is a person who is oriented toward cooperation with others. She says that she needs to explore, meet with people. Without that she would not be able to deliver quality content. YouTube is associated with online activity, but most of her actions take place in the real world (roughly 25% vs 75%). Once, that proportion was inverted, but that is changing with the growth of her business.

She makes decisions by listening to her intuition. "*Because that doesn't fail me.*"

Red Lipstick Monster carefully maintains her privacy. If she reveals something from her private life, she does so quite intentionally. She does not meet viewers socially. "*Being on my own terms. Clear boundaries between personal life and work. It's always been that way.*"

The YouTuber also cares for her visual identity (her logo, the distinctive opening of her makeup tutorials).

Changes in Her Personal Brand

The main values of Red Lipstick Monster's personal brand have been consistent. In the process of shaping the brand, there were no major breakthroughs or sudden changes. The YouTuber does mention, however, that now she is much more self-confident. Once, she was more timid, but now she is more bold: "*I am more myself.*"

At first, she did not know how to act and sought solutions and inspiration. Now she feels that there are no limits, and she is free and fulfilled. "*At first, I drew on others, recycled, but over the course of time I gained confidence and created my own individual style. I don't look back, because I have more trust in myself.*"

Red Lipstick Monster also feels more mature, has concrete plans for the future and knows what she wants. This is probably clearly visible to viewers and is part of the value of her brand.

Strategic Goals

Red Lipstick Monster's dream is to launch her own line of cosmetics. "*At the present moment, this is the biggest challenge. Many years of work. I don't like something if it is easy.*" She wants to achieve this within ten years. The goal is also to open a store: "*a real store with a sign.*" First, however, she plans to open an online store.

Target Group
The target group for her YouTube channel is people interested in makeup, especially young women. Red Lipstick Monster monitors the demographic indicators about her viewers. The largest group is people aged 18–25, then those under 18, and in third place, over 25 years of age.

The YouTuber would like to have viewers only over the age of 18. She believes that younger people do not understand what she shows. *"Dream: 18+ and for no one under. I consciously create my content. Young people like popular, distinctive people. YouTube is in. They don't understand what I'm saying."*

Red Lipstick Monster also pays attention to the media (*"Traditional media, but more serious, more respected ones, like* Wyborcza*"* [a respected national newspaper]) as well as potential business partners.

Benchmarks and Models
Her only model is American YouTuber Michelle Phan (beauty, fashion, lifestyle). Why? *"She has an enchanting personality, her heart on her sleeve, great business partners."*

Red Lipstick Monster meets with other YouTubers; they share experiences and inspire each other (but these are not YouTubers in the beauty category, who she says are rather closed individuals).

Measures of the Personal Brand Image
Red Lipstick Monster is aware of her image in the target group. A few years ago, her friend conducted a market research study on the perception of Red Lipstick Monster for her MA thesis in Public Relations. The results confirmed what the YouTuber knew intuitively.

Later, Red Lipstick Monster herself conducted research on the online community regarding the associations she evokes. Again, it turned out that the results were consistent with expectations: *"All the most important traits."*

Currently, the YouTuber is engaged in active dialog with her viewers, reads their comments and asks for concrete feedback. This gives her a current overview of how she is perceived.

Factors in Success and Failure
In Red Lipstick Monster's opinion, the most important factor in success is to know what means you're going to use to go in the direction you have set

out: "*You don't necessarily have to know what's at the end of the road, but you do have to have intermediate goals, work hard, and have a vision.*" It is essential thus to decide on goals and means, so that the actions will be coherent and consistent. One can overcome one's own barriers, but it should be done carefully and with some thought.

Red Lipstick Monster says that she is the only beauty vlogger who offers something more than just makeup tutorials, for example, lifestyle content. That may also have contributed to her success.

Of course, her media presence is important: "*You can give five different people the same content, and they'll have different viewer statistics.*"

Factors affecting failure are recycling and a lack of originality. One cannot copy anyone else's solutions: "*Your work has to be real, because if it isn't coherent and authentic there won't be any enthusiasm.*"

Trends and View of the Future in the Context of Building Her Personal Brand
Red Lipstick Monster will consistently build her personal brand. She does not see any particular trends in this area. She says that joy is important: "*Joy, you are yourself and you don't see anything special or extraordinary. It is important to have greater self-awareness, to understand yourself. Trust yourself.*"

Case Study: Jaś Dąbrowski

Case study: Jaś Dąbrowski (Jan Dąbrowski, age 20)
Interview date: January 28, 2016

History of the YouTuber
The history of YouTuber Jaś Dąbrowski began a few years ago. At that time, he was interested in computer graphics and took part in discussion forums, on which he showed his work. After a while, he began to watch YouTubers. He was then noticed by Rock & Rojo. Next, he began to cooperate with YouTuber skkf. He made graphics for skkf's YouTube channel. After some time, skkf invited Jaś to take part in a live stream during which they would play computer games. It turned out that people liked Jaś Dąbrowski and asked where they could find him. That provided the impulse to start recording his own videos.

At that time (around 2–3 years ago) Minecraft was very popular, so Jaś Dąbrowski began creating videos based on this game. He offered viewers something fresh and original. Usually, players would show how they build objects in Minecraft, but Jaś Dąbrowski created fictional stories. These were well received, and the YouTuber expanded his work, taking up new topics and also beginning to create commercial projects in other areas.

Jaś Dąbrowski broadly diversified his business activities. Aside from his activity on YouTube, he has a Minecraft game server (www.jasmc.pl), runs a clothing company, JDabrowsky Wear, and organizes summer camps for youth, TereCamp.

Jaś Dąbrowski noticed that viewers have a need to identify with him, asking him, for example, whether it was possible to buy clothing branded with his name. When he set up his clothing business, he turned to the company Kapsel for personalization of shirts. After some time, he decided to get more involved in this area, especially as creating a clothing brand had been one of his dreams. He wanted to do so professionally, with high-quality and at the same time attractive clothing. He established his own sewing workshop, and this season (in 2016) began to cooperate with Sara Pisak to create a collection for girls (he designs clothing for boys himself).

The YouTuber also organizes holidays for youth (TereCamp). As soon as he realized that he had fans who wanted to meet him and at the same time spend their school holidays in an interesting way, he created an appropriate product for them.

Jaś Dąbrowski also has his own radio program on Polish Radio Four, which addresses topics of interest to youth (problems with school, games, the Internet).

His brother helps him with many things, dealing with technical, organizational and legal questions. Of course, he also uses the help of professionals (for example, lawyers and educators).

The YouTuber has experience cooperating with many brands, including Coca-Cola, Tesco for schools, Nestlé (Kaktus ice cream), PlayStation, Hasbro, Disney and Play. *"Brands are glad to work with me, because I'm nice and well-behaved. I'm a safe option, working with me doesn't hurt."* Jaś Dąbrowski is satisfied with this cooperation, because it builds up his finances, which allows him to do creative work professionally (for example, he can hire a good camera operator).

For Jaś Dąbrowski, one of his greatest successes was to voice a character in the dubbed Polish version of the movie *Zootopia*. This was also a dream come true for him. He received many awards for his work (for example, for the "Kaktus Republic" campaign). The Bravoora award from the magazine Bravo for the greatest Internet star of 2015 was important. Jaś Dąbrowski says, however, that: "*I don't want to call myself a star. On YouTube, the creator is under the viewers. The viewers decide. But it's a nice reward, because it shows that people trust me a lot and really support me. I've got a bunch of loyal fans, viewers.*"

The YouTuber's Perspective on Personal Branding: Associations, Understanding, Relevance
Jaś Dąbrowski associates a personal brand with an image, that which people perceive, what they associate him with and how. His personal brand is very important to him:

> *My brand is my whole person. Whether or not people watch me depends on what my brand is. People watch YouTube not just because of the videos, but also because of what you are. If I show a bad side of me or do something bad, people won't want to watch me... they'll think I'm not the cool dude I look like, but that I'm just trying to pose.*

The YouTuber is aware that while, for example, there are millions of videos about Minecraft, it is his personality (personal brand) that gives the recordings their value and meaning: "*The content is less important than who stands behind it.*"

He regards every subscription he receives as his personal success, in large part resulting from his personal brand (in 2016 there were over 830,000). He is glad that the number of subscriptions is constantly growing.

Perception of His Own Personal Brand
"*I am nice and well-behaved, with a sense of humor that comes across to viewers. I'm warm inside and tell jokes I know. People watch me when they're on their way to school and feeling sad. There's no pressure, it's neat and natural.*' The terms that Jaś Dąbrowski mentions when asked about his image are close, friend, doesn't keep a distance, spontaneous, real. "*My image is built on a real character, I don't pretend to be anyone else (I pretend to be Iron Man or the Hulk, but that's something else – I'm playing a role then)*"; the YouTuber is fully satisfied with his image.

The Practice of Shaping His Personal Brand: Methods and Tools

Natural behavior, being in harmony with yourself: "*I don't show anything off, I don't whitewash anything. People talking with me on vacation see that I'm for real.*"

Polite behavior: "*I'm built on being nice and well-behaved, I don't swear, I'm not vulgar or aggressive. My viewers' parents see that and appreciate it.*"

Neat appearance: "*I'm an authority for kids, I can't show up dirty.*"

In everything he does, Jaś Dąbrowski strives to achieve the highest quality. For his activity on YouTube, this means that he makes fewer videos but they are well-crafted: "*I won't throw up 100 episodes a week, but have only two that are well-edited.*"

In the case of his clothing company, he uses his own sewing workshop. The clothing is more expensive, but high quality: "*People buy it because of me, but also because of the quality and design.*" TereCamp offers interesting activities for youth with professional supervision. Participants include Jaś Dąbrowski himself, because he knows that young people come to the camp to meet him.

High quality means also having the trust of viewers and of their parents: "*When I do something, it's done well enough that they won't be disappointed. I do everything legally and safely.*"

Transparency and honesty—the YouTuber does not hide that he works with businesses, but at the same time knows that his personality endorses certain products or services: "*If some publisher sends me a book and asks me to say it's my favorite book, I don't agree. I can only say that I got it and read it. But there are fewer and fewer situations like that. Companies are giving up bad practices.*"

Jaś Dąbrowski is also intentionally close to his public, and also makes selected areas of his private life available; for example, he shows his home. He meets with fans during TereCamp and industry festivities (for example, New Winter Game). He presents coherent content having to do with computer games, figures from pop culture and hobbies. Creativity, creatively making trends, originality and adding something from himself are important traits for him. Being current is also important, keeping a finger on the pulse of what's going on.

Changes in His Personal Brand

There have been no significant changes in Jaś Dąbrowski's image (there was neither a need nor a desire for a rebranding). Doubtless, however, is that over the course of time the YouTuber has grown more mature, more self-confident, more professional. He is still young (20 years old), and began his activity on YouTube as a teenager. Changes in his image are thus inevitable, but are evolutionary in character.

Strategic Goals

Jaś Dąbrowski strives to develop the success of his YouTube channel and to have a growing number of subscribers. It is important for him to always do what he is passionate about. He wants to develop in various areas, for example, to work more with Disney on dubbing films. He also plans to develop his businesses (as mentioned above, he is gradually developing his clothing brand).

Target Group

The target group for Jaś Dąbrowski's YouTube channel is young people. Statistics show that more of them are female. The YouTuber knows his target group well. He is constantly seeking so-called insights, or consumer preferences, which the consumer does not show directly. Thanks to that, the content he shows corresponds to the interests of his viewers: "*I know that if I record something about a bicycle, it will get a lot of views.*"

Jaś tries to meet the expectations of his public and at the same time remain true to himself: "*I take their feedback and average it out, so that I have fun and am natural and they get what they want.*"

Jaś Dąbrowski's public is highly engaged. An example might be when the YouTuber began working with Sprite, and viewers spontaneously sent him pictures of themselves posing with the company's products.

An important part of the target group is viewers' parents—it is they, after all, who decide or partially decide which summer camp their child will go to. Of course, important target groups also include potential advertisers and business partners.

Benchmarks and Models

In the gaming category, Jaś Dąbrowski is inspired by YouTubers from abroad (that is, he appreciates PewDiePie, who is a trendsetter in this area). He declares that he would rather not watch Polish YouTubers in the gaming category, because he does not want to commit unintentional plagiarism and does not want to draw on others' ideas.

The source of general inspiration for him is Włodek Markowicz—it was he who inspired Jaś Dąbrowski to show his home. The YouTuber appreciates his team Terefere, who are also a source of inspiration.

Measures of the Personal Brand Image
Jaś Dąbrowski does not conduct any formal measurements of his personal brand image. He is, however, in constant contact with his viewers: "*My channel is based on relationships.*" Thus, he knows how he is perceived. He also has insights about his image from the companies he works with[2]: "*Friends tell me how things look from their point of view, parents of viewers tell me.*"

Factors in Success and Failure
Looking after quality and constantly maintaining high quality is what makes it possible to build a loyal base of viewers waiting for the next video. The ability to build close relationships with viewers, based on trust from both sides is key here. It is essential to listen to people and keep in close contact with them. Thanks to this, Jaś Dąbrowski knows what his viewers expect, and can accommodate them. The YouTuber dedicates a lot of time towards contact with the public on Facebook. He asks for feedback, reads comments, takes short polls. At TereCamp he has close, direct contact with the participants—his fans.

The factors in success include well-organized and systematic work. A YouTuber has to constantly take care to maintain viewers' interest: "*I can't really take a break, because that would have a negative impact on views and the engagement of viewers.*"

Knowing and having a good sense of trends plays an important role. It isn't enough, however, to simply follow trends—it is important to creatively modify them, to add something creative from oneself. Image coherence is essential, which can be reached, for example, through working with companies that are well-suited in terms of image.

What can lead to failure is a lack of authenticity, not knowing viewers' expectations, lack of contact with viewers, as well as doing unfashionable things.

Jaś experienced failure in one of his undertakings. Together with DJ Remo he recorded a single on CD (guest appearance). The YouTuber's public did not like this. Why not? Jaś commented: '*I, a calm, well-behaved guy, appeared in a dance music video, boom-boom, and they felt that it was not for me, not my style and not my type of music. It turned out that viewers did not accept the inconsistency. Viewers know me. They know what kind of music I listen to. That was a bucket of cold water.'*

Trends and View of the Future in the Context of Building His Personal Brand
Jaś Dąbrowski says that he wants to grow up with his viewers. He relies on intuition and spontaneity. He is aware that in a year or two, his audience will expect more mature content: *"The image in the future – be myself. And what I'll be we'll see in a few years. Up until now I've followed along viewers' needs, without any great plans. It just worked out on its own."*

Case Study: Wapniak

Case study: Wapniak (Maciej Wapiński, age 25)
Date of interview: February 15, 2016

History of the YouTuber
On his web page, he writes about himself as follows:

> *I am the creator of two channels: Wapniak and Man Up Polska. On the first one, I focus on positive and practical personal development and show mental trans-formation through fun. At first, I developed my self-confidence by doing crazy things, now I show how you can enjoy life being open and conscious. On the second channel, I focus on physical development. I show physical training, diets and promote a healthy lifestyle.* (http://wapniak.pl/)

Wapniak began his activity on YouTube in 2013. He uploaded his first video on January 5, 2013. He works now on mental and physical development, cross-fit training, diet (the Samurai and Paleo diets). Currently, there are diverse topics on his channel; we can find, for example, a series "From zero to hero – Wapniak" (Become a hero in every field), "Automotive – from zero to master driver", "Travel", "Happy Life", "Wealth – investing – money", "Militaria – weapons – shooting", "Politics", and "Poker isn't gambling." The diversity of topics is linked to Wapniak's own wide interests, his desire to explore many facets of life and to make his dreams come true. He used to work on entertainment, but now his goal is to build a channel with more serious, valuable content.

Wapniak began his activity on YouTube because of the following factors that came together for him: a desire to overcome shyness, a desire to get out among people, and a lack of interest in his studies (finance and accounting). An important motivation was also a desire to be attractive to women. As he himself says, *"I was that guy holding a beer, leaning against the wall and watching how others were having fun. I watched foreign advice films about how to pick up girls."*

He decided to change that. Making prank videos in which he made jokes or fooled people, was supposed to be a kind of self-therapy. It demanded confidence, courage and the ability to go beyond his comfort zone.

Wapniak's great success in terms of viewership (with ca. 3.5 million views) was the video *Make me an ice cream?*[3], in which he approaches strangers at a mall and asks them whether they could make him an ice cream. After a moment of surprise (the Polish original is a potentially lewd double-entendre), he explained that he was talking about making an ice cream from the vending machine nearby, which he could not do himself, because his arm was in a sling.

Of course, this kind of video reached a particular group of viewers and created a certain image of the filmmaker. As soon as Wapniak felt that he no longer cared for this image, he encountered many problems with rebranding and changing his target group.

He counts making a joke with then Polish president Bronisław Komorowski during his re-election campaign as one of his greatest successes. Wapniak posed for a picture with him, showing the initials of Janusz Korwin-Mikke, a rival candidate (Wapniak 2015). He now recognizes that as proof that he had reached his goal of overcoming his shyness.

The YouTuber's Perspective on Personal Branding: Associations, Understanding, Relevance

In Wapniak's view, a personal brand is the creation of a particular person, their logo and their story. Shaping a brand is a long-term process, which requires a lot of engagement. Wapniak also came to feel how a personal brand can be a *"pigeon hole that it is hard to escape, but that characterizes a given person, their work and activities."*

A personal brand is very important; success depends on it. On the Internet it's essential to create a strong brand, to be distinctive, extraordinary: *"People are drawn to a concrete person, a brand. They aren't drawn to FitnessClub S4, but only to Michał Szostak."*

Perception of His Own Personal Brand
The hero of this study is aware that his beginnings in social media created a particular, highly distinctive image: *"Once: fat, funny Wapniak, now the Wapniak who works out and develops himself. A satisfied, positive guy who helps others with personal development. He'll be an expert."* It should be mentioned that when he started his online activity he was not aware of what the consequences for his image would be.

Practice of Shaping His Personal Brand: Methods and Tools
Because Wapniak is undergoing an image change, it is worth comparing his methods when he started on YouTube to those he uses now.

At first, he recorded pranks—he played unsophisticated jokes on people and put the videos up on YouTube. Wapniak had no set plan or strategy then, he did what he thought was funny and might increase his popularity.

Now, his activity is based on certain methods:

(a) presentation of the road to success in a given area under the general slogan "from zero to hero" (from a complete novice to a particular level)

(b) broad range of diverse topic areas

(c) use of the example of himself—Wapniak himself experiences what he is telling viewers about

(d) striving toward expertise

(e) showing the effects of his activities (for example, if he shows some exercises in the gym, he also needs to show his muscles), and the recommendations of other people, thanks to which the YouTuber is perceived as effective and trustworthy

(f) acting and dressing in an easy and laid-back way.

As mentioned at the beginning of the case study, Wapniak addresses a very wide and diverse range of topics. He is not, however, worried about becoming spread too thin or lacking distinctiveness, because he, as a personality, is the common denominator in all the work.

This has to do with coherence, which Wapniak understands as being in harmony with yourself: *"Coherence – that's being close to yourself. My life, I show my own life, how I feel is very important for me both on the inside and outside, for example healthy intestines and stomach."*

Wapniak to a large degree believes in his intuition. He does take care to not let his brand influence his personal life, and consciously keeps them apart. For example, even if he feels that he is a diet expert, he does not bring that over to the making breakfast for his girlfriend. *"You have to be a partner, and not an expert."*

Changes in His Personal Brand

"Crossing over from being a joker to a personal development guy is freaking insane. Rebranding is really hard. You get a lot of hate from people. People are like horses wearing blinders, they only see one thing and don't want anything else, they don't accept change"— this is how Wapniak sees his experience related to changing the character of his work on YouTube.

As previously mentioned, Wapniak's earlier image was created incidentally, impulsively, unintentionally: *"I put videos up on the Internet and checked the views and comments to see if people liked them, if I should make more."*

Over time, Wapniak noticed that the particular image and video topics strictly limited his earning potential on YouTube: *"It wasn't a favorable image in terms of finding advertising work. No one wants to work with a guy who asks people in a mall if they'll 'make me an ice cream.' "* The second motivation was the realization that something that was meant to be funny (though perhaps not in the best taste), was beginning to affect people too much and there were a number of imitators—similar videos appeared, for example, *Hold my balls*.[4]

A very important matter was also the process of growing more emotionally mature and beginning to work out in the gym: *"I changed as a person, the old life didn't suit me anymore. Instead of boozing it up on Friday, I go to the gym."*

The best summary for his process of change is in his own words: *"Now people watch me and don't see a joker, not the homie Wapniak, but just Mr. Wapniak."*

Strategic Goals

At first, the goal of Wapniak's online activity was to overcome his shyness. After a certain time, he began to focus on business goals—he wanted to earn money from what he did on YouTube.

> *A kind of self-therapy, earning a little bit of money. I earned PLN 900 and felt like a king, I was a student, lived in the dorm, and we bought so much booze. . . That's*

what I needed then. As soon as I got anything from YouTube it went straight to alcohol, the vegetation was terrible, but that's what I needed then.

His initial goals fully achieved, Wapniak's goals now include:

(a) monetizing his activity, for example, by creating a program *How to overcome shyness in 30 days* or through consulting work as a personal trainer
(b) personal satisfaction
(c) gaining and holding the interest of viewers
(d) inspiring viewers, to be a kind of mentor and help people (*"I like it when people write me e-mails to thank me: 'I had suicidal thoughts, but I watched your videos, I feel like living and am going on vacation.'"*).

Target Group
When he started his activity on YouTube, Wapniak did not think about who was watching him. The target group was not intentionally chosen. Later he became aware that it was mostly very young people, middle-schoolers, for whom he was an authority: *"For sure he drinks beer in front of the cops, the dude's got balls. Pictures, autographs, praise from the kids."*

Wapniak is aware that for viewers a change in his profile could come as a shock. Old viewers came back and did not get what they wanted (entertainment, prank videos). Some of his viewers left (around 20,000), the number of views went down as did the demographics of his viewers. The YouTuber says, however, that he would rather have a smaller but more conscious audience looking for quality: *"I ran away from the rat race after subscription numbers at the cost of reduced quality."*

The current period can be described as a transition between a young public interested in pranks to a more sophisticated, more mature public, interested in what's broadly understood as development. Wapniak himself emphasizes that he wants to create his public and is aware that what he is doing now demands a complete change of his public's profile.

Potential advertisers and business partners are also an important group that Wapniak takes into consideration when thinking about his work.

Benchmarks and Models
For his YouTube materials, Wapniak takes inspiration from the international travel channel High On Life. He says, however, that cooperation with its creators is out of reach for now, and he would rather be a Polish version of

them than to work with them. He also admires the owner of the channel Casey Neistat.

Wapniak decides himself about the selection of topics, with advice from his camera operator and his girlfriend. The YouTuber has various contacts with experts in areas he is interested in (for example, dietetics) and learns from them; this also includes courses and training seminars in the real world.

Measures of the Personal Brand Image
Wapniak does not conduct any systematic analysis of his image, but through reading comments on the videos he is aware of how he is received. He knows that it is too early to do research, because it can be expected that his image will have values from the past "*I know that they are under 18 and want "*Make me an ice cream 2.*"

Factors in Success and Failure
In Wapniak's view, the factors in success are above all:

(a) originality, distinctiveness
(b) passion, doing what you love
(c) authenticity, being in harmony with yourself
(d) consistency, striving toward goals
(e) coherence
(f) working hard, being systematic
(g) contact with the public, interacting with them (Wapniak answers emails and corresponds with viewers).

What leads to failure is not being systematic, uninteresting content, a YouTuber losing touch with reality (with how viewers live and what they are interested in).

Trends and View of the Future in the Context of Building His Personal Brand
Wapniak believes that one cannot rely on trends, only on one's own inner voice and intuition: "*Don't do what's currently popular, only do what you love.*" When it comes to the development of his personal brand, he would like it to contain stronger traits of an expert. He says, however, that "*I feel free, maybe in five years I'll change.*" He thus leaves the path open to following what intuition tells him.

Summary of the Qualitative Part

All respondents are aware of the huge role that a personal brand plays on YouTube. They are convinced that the creator of the content, and how he or she speaks, is many times more important than the content itself. Respondents believe that a well-created personal brand is the decisive factor in success, and is important in setting a given person apart from the countless number of other YouTubers. At the same time, all the respondents emphasize that to build a credible and recognizable personal brand, it is important to be oneself and listen to one's heart and intuition.

RESEARCH RESULTS: QUANTITATIVE PART

In the quantitative part of the research regarding selected aspects of creating a personal brand using social media, in particular YouTube, two groups of respondents were surveyed—young people (age 18–34) from Poland and from the United States. The answers given to specific questions are presented below.

Awareness of and Associations with the Term "Personal Branding"

The research showed that 45% of young Poles and 55% of young Americans had come across the term "personal branding." Fewer than 30% of the sample in each country had never heard of the term. Interestingly, a significant percentage (19% in the United States, and 27% in Poland) answered "Difficult to say / Not sure." This may signify that the topic is only beginning to enter into their lives: they are not familiar enough with the term to answer unambiguously "yes", but at the same time may have encountered the term "personal branding" (to a small degree) (Fig. 5.6).

There is a statistically significant correlation between the country the respondents are from and the awareness of the term "personal branding", as is illustrated in Table 5.14.

People who had come across the term before were asked what it means to them, and those who had not encountered the term before were asked to list what associations the term raises. Many of the respondents associated this term with creating one's own image using social media. For example:

> It is a brand that we create by writing a blog, running a fan page, or a Pinterest profile. (Poland, female, age 30–34).

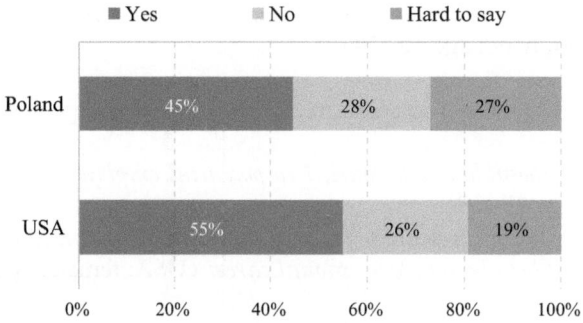

Fig. 5.6 Awareness of the term "personal branding" ($N = 504$ (Poland); $N = 500$ (USA), entire sample. Source: Own research)

Table 5.14 Correlation between country of origin and awareness of the term "personal branding"

Statistical test	Poland vs. USA		
	χ^2	df	p
Pearson's χ^2	12.60140	$df = 2$	$p = 0.00184$
ML χ^2	12.64447	$df = 2$	$p = 0.00180$

Source: Own calculations
df degrees of freedom

Creating unique content, which makes people following you on social media remember you (USA, male, age 18–24).
Caring for your own image by using the Internet. (Poland, female, age 25–29).
Creating an identity on the Internet that lets others easily distinguish the content you put up (USA, male, age 25–29).

Some of those studied believed that a personal brand is created constantly (through activities and behaviors), not necessarily by using social media for this purpose.

A personal brand is a concrete person and everything associated with them, everything that you could say about them. (Poland, female, age 19–24).

For some people, though, a personal brand means an image in the eyes of others.

What people think about you, for example when you walk into a room.
(Poland, male, age 18–24).

A personal brand is also associated with business and professional work.

It makes it possible to sell yourself to potential employers or clients (USA,
male, age 25–29).
*Using your online presence to create a coherent brand, an image of yourself
that will help in your professional career* (USA, female, age 30–34).

Other respondents were of the opinion that a personal brand is something that mainly celebrities create with the help of public relations experts.
There were also associations with the FMCG (fast-moving consumer
goods) industry: a personal brand was thought to be a popular, frequently
purchased product brand.

A brand preferred by a particular person (Poland, male, age 30–34).
A brand that is adapted to my expectations (USA, male, age 18–24).

The association with product endorsements also appeared.

*For example, someone produces bags and endorses them with their first and
last name.* (Poland, female, age 30–34).

Respondents were also presented with a short definition of personal
branding and asked whether they had heard that way of describing it before.
The definition was written by the author of this work based on the subject
literature (cf. Malinowska-Parzydło, 2015, pp. 19, 74; McNally & Speak,
2003, p. 4; Montoya & Vandehey, 2005, pp. 11–12; Rampersad, 2008,
pp. 34–37; Schawbel, 2010, p. 5; Trzeciak, 2015, p. 21; Wojtaszczyk &
Maszewski, 2014, pp. 456), his own considerations, as well as the results of
the qualitative research. The definition offered was the following:

**Personal branding is your image – this is how you are perceived by
others. Creating it is a <u>strategy</u> for building your reputation and improv-
ing how others perceive you. One way to build your personal brand is to
<u>intentionally</u> communicate specific content in social media.**

It turned out that 50% of Poles and 67% of Americans surveyed had heard
of personal branding described in this way (Fig. 5.7).

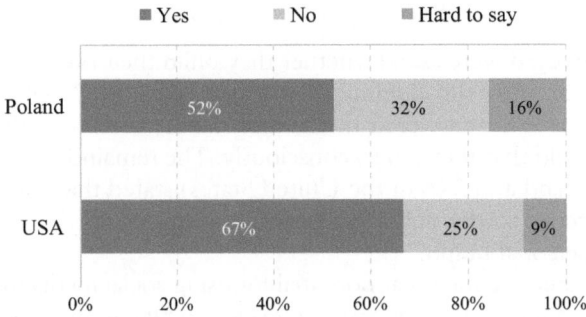

Fig. 5.7 Familiarity with the term "personal branding" in accordance with the definition provided ($N = 504$ (Poland); $N = 500$ (USA), entire sample. Source: Own research)

Table 5.15 Correlation between country of origin and familiarity with the term "personal branding" in accordance with the definition provided

Statistical test	Poland vs. USA		
	χ^2	df	p
Pearson's χ^2	23.24837	df = 2	p = 0.00001
ML χ^2	23.43174	df = 2	p = 0.00001

Source: Own research

There exists a statistically significant correlation between country of origin of the respondents and their familiarity with the term "personal branding" in accordance with the provided definition, as is illustrated in Table 5.15.

That more people responded that they had come across the term after reading the definition than did in the case of having no definition is natural. Frequently, presentation of a description of some phenomenon to a respondent causes them to begin to have better recall.

In the next questions regarding personal branding, respondents were asked to respond to the above definition. Because of this, one can state that the participants' responses regard the same aspects of building a personal brand as in this work.

Building a Personal Brand

All those surveyed were asked whether they build their own personal brand in accordance with the definition provided: 62% of Poles and 47% of Americans surveyed answered in the affirmative, of which 22% and 23% respectively said that they did so consciously. The remainder (40% of young people in Poland and 24% in the United States) stated that they build their brand according to the definition provided, but did not know that this is building a personal brand.

One can then see the great potential for using social media in this area in the future, if these individuals were to decide to take up more strategic and methodical action (Fig. 5.8).

There exists a statistically significant correlation between the country of origin of respondents and building a personal brand, as is shown in Table 5.16.

Those respondents who consciously build their personal brand were asked to what extent they are satisfied with what they have undertaken in this regard. Around two-thirds of respondents (66% in Poland, 64% in the

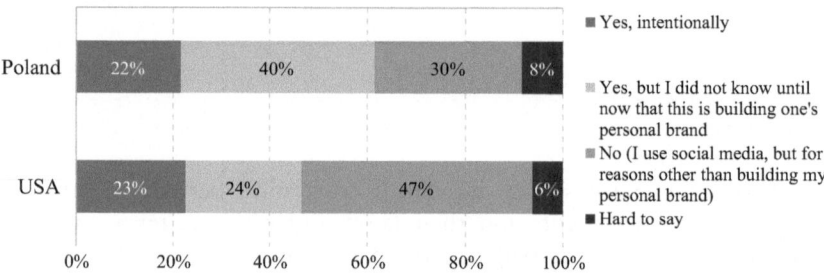

Fig. 5.8 Building a personal brand according to the definition provided ($N = 504$ (Poland); $N = 500$ (USA), entire sample. Source: Own research)

Table 5.16 Correlation between country of origin and building a personal brand

Statistical test	Poland vs. USA		
	χ^2	df	p
Pearson's χ^2	40.33913	$df = 3$	$p = 0.00000$
ML χ^2	40.71224	$df = 3$	$p = 0.00000$

Source: Own research

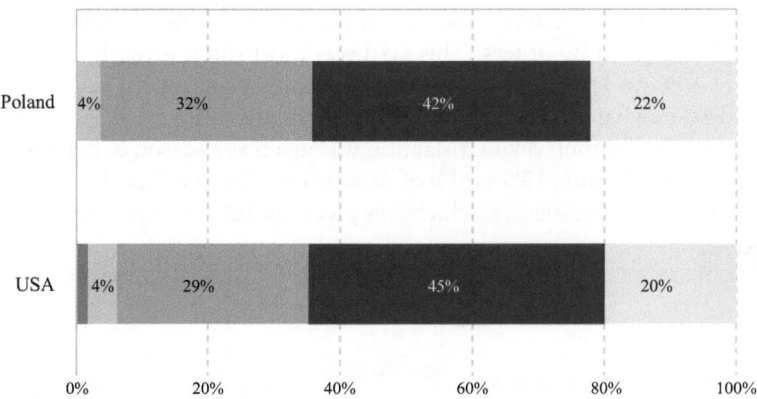

- ■ 1 (Very dissatisfied)
- ▨ 2 (Somewhat dissatisfied)
- ▩ 3 (Neutral)
- ■ 4 (Somewhat satisfied)
- ▨ 5 (Very satisfied)

Fig. 5.9 Satisfaction with actions related to building a personal brand ($N = 109$ (Poland); $N = 113$ (USA), persons consciously building their personal brand. Source: Own research)

Table 5.17 Correlation between country of origin and satisfaction with actions undertaken to develop a personal brand	Statistical tool	Poland vs. USA		
		χ^2	df	p
	Pearson's χ^2	6.271589	$df = 4$	$p = 0.17976$
	ML χ^2	7.406436	$df = 4$	$p = 0.11591$

Source: Own research

United States) are satisfied with the actions they have undertaken, and only a small percentage (under 5%) are unsatisfied. The remainder do not have a specific opinion (Fig. 5.9).

There is no statistically significant correlation between the country of origin of respondents and their level of satisfaction with actions undertaken to develop their own brand, as illustrated in Table 5.17.

Goals of Building a Personal Brand

Individuals who said that they build their personal brand (both consciously and unconsciously) were asked why they do so and what they want to achieve. These were open questions.

Figure 5.10 below shows the coded responses.

In both countries, appearing in first place was a rather general goal—to be well-perceived by others. This goal was most often given by Americans (nearly 40% vs. 16% of Poles). The next goal is professional success, mentioned somewhat more frequently by Americans (23% vs. 15% of Poles). Interestingly, for their own satisfaction was given as a reason decidedly more frequently in Poland (13% vs. 1% of Americans). The next goal was meeting goals and achieving success, which was given by 10% of respondents in each

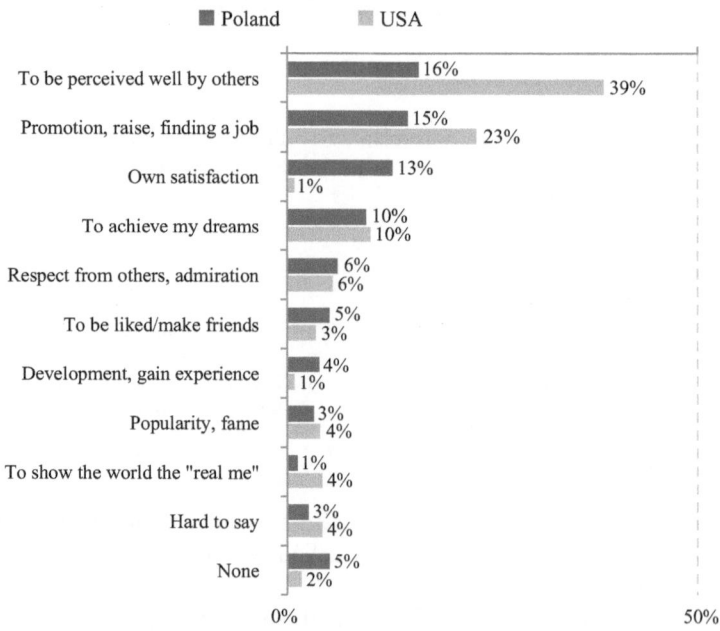

Fig. 5.10   Goals of building a personal brand. Coded responses to open questions ($N = 310$ (Poland); $N = 233$ (USA), individuals build a personal brand. Source: Own research. * The chart shows answers that were given by at least 3% of respondents in at least one country)

country. The remaining goals were mentioned by less than 10% of respondents.

A few selected responses are given below.

> *I want to get a promotion this way.* (Poland, male, age 30–34)
> *Maybe I can find friends or a great job.* (Poland, female, age 25–29)
> *To build my brand and make money.* (USA, male, age 18–24)
> *I want to be a surgeon. My goal is to make a good impression and a good reputation.* (USA, female, age 18–24)
> *So people will see me as I am, and not just from what they hear from other people.* (Poland, female, age 18–24)
> *I want to be a legend.* (USA, male, age 25–29)

Ways of Building a Personal Brand

Young people building a personal brand were asked in what way they do so, what activities they undertake. This was an open question, and Fig. 5.11 below shows the coded responses.

Young people shaping their personal brand more frequently answered that they do so by posting and making comments on social media (34% of Poles and 44% of Americans). Ten percent in each country stated that they put their picture up on social media. It is worth mentioning that 11% of those surveyed in each country said that they built their personal brand by "being authentic, being themselves" (which is in line with the statements of Polish YouTubers in the qualitative part, that being oneself is the key to creating a personal brand).

The remaining ways of building a personal brand were mentioned by less than 10% of respondents, but it is worth mentioning that Americans also spoke of networking, posting consistent information about oneself on all social media and generally presenting oneself as a professional. Poles either did not mention these aspects or do them less frequently.

A few selected responses are presented below.

> *I am always honest, don't lie, try to listen to everyone and treat them with respect.* (Poland, male, age 18–24).
> *I am active on Twitter and Instagram. I also have my own web page.* (USA, female, age 25–29).

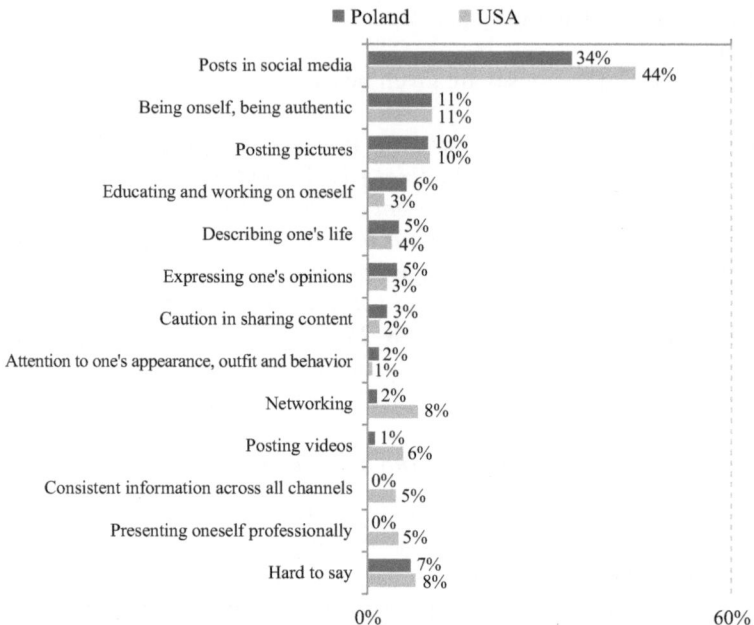

Fig. 5.11 Ways of shaping a personal brand. Coded answers to open questions (N = 310 (Poland); N = 233 (USA), individuals building a personal brand. Source: own research. * The chart shows answers that were given by at least 3% of respondents in at least one country)

> *I carefully choose what I post, how often I post, and try to maintain a balance between personal and professional topics.* (USA, male, age 25–29).
>
> *I have a blog, post interesting things on Facebook, Instagram and Pinterest. I have a profile on LinkedIn.* (Poland, female, age 18–24).
>
> *I make comments and share on forums.* (Poland, male, age 18–24).
>
> *I build my brand through my style, the kind of pictures I post on Facebook, as well as the kind of content I put online.* (USA, female, age 25–29).

Use of Social Media to Build a Personal Brand

Individuals building their personal brand were asked to indicate which social media they use for this purpose. It was made clear in the question that this was about using a given medium for building a personal brand, and not about use in general.

In both countries, the unquestioned leader turned out to be Facebook, which 86% of Poles and 77% of Americans use to build their personal brand. In second place in Poland, although with a significantly lower number of answers, was YouTube (30%) and in third place, Google+ (27%).

In the United States, in second place was Instagram (49%), and in third place, LinkedIn (37%). YouTube was used for building a personal brand by 25% of those surveyed. This is somewhat lower than in Poland, but other services turned out to be more popular.

Also noteworthy is the difference between Facebook and YouTube. Among individuals who use Facebook and are building their personal brand, a substantial percentage (85% in the United States, 91% in Poland) use it to build their personal brand. In the case of YouTube, this percentage was 25% and 30% respectively. Of course, this results from the different character of these media, but also from the fact that using YouTube to build a personal brand requires greater engagement and preparation (Fig. 5.12).

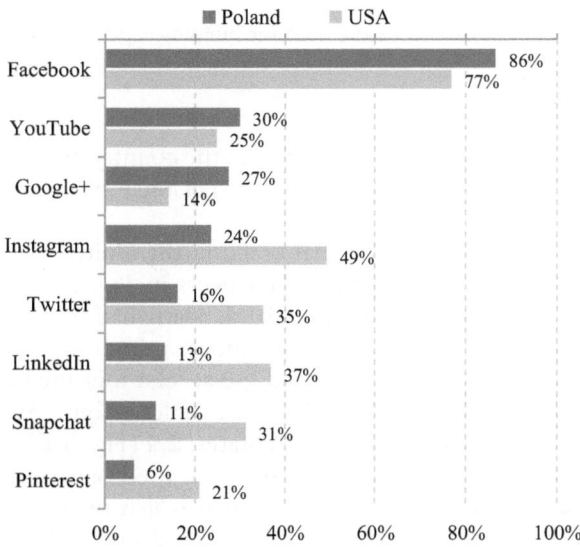

Fig. 5.12 Social media used to build a personal brand ($N = 310$ (Poland); $N = 233$ (USA), individuals building a personal brand. Source: Own research)

Table 5.18 Correlation between country of origin of respondents and use of YouTube to build a personal brand

Statistical tool	Poland vs. USA (YouTube)		
	χ^2	df	p
Pearson's χ^2	1.728369	$df = 1$	$p = 0.18862$
ML χ^2	1.739622	$df = 1$	$p = 0.18719$

Source: Own research

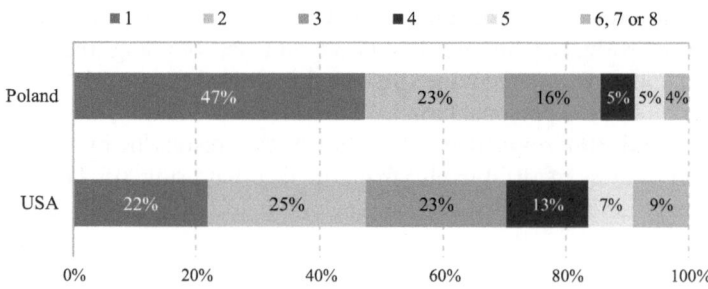

Fig. 5.13 Number of social media used for building a personal brand ($N = 310$ (Poland); $N = 233$ (USA), individuals building a personal brand. Source: Own research)

No significant correlation exists between the country of origin of respondents and use of YouTube to build a personal brand, as shown in Table 5.18.

Young people creating a personal brand in the United States use more social media for this purpose than their peers in Poland. Among young people creating a personal brand in Poland, nearly half (47%) use only one medium. In the United States, the percentage using only one medium is 22%. In Poland, 14% of those surveyed use at least four media, whereas in the United States 29% of respondents use at least four. Average use in Poland is 2.1 media, and in the United States, 2.9 (Fig. 5.13).

Because a certain portion of those surveyed used only one medium for building a personal brand, it was ascertained which medium that was. In Poland, first place was held by Facebook (78%), second by YouTube (10%), while the remaining media all were under 5%. In the United States, Facebook also turned out to be the most frequently used medium for building a personal brand, but with a weaker result than in Poland (53%), while in second place was LinkedIn (20%), and third, YouTube (8%).

Use of YouTube for Building a Personal Brand

Young Poles and Americans who use YouTube to build their personal brand were asked in what way they do so, what benefits does YouTube provide and what are its weak points in building a personal brand. These were open questions.

As can be seen in Fig. 5.14, the most frequent activity is recording and posting videos. What is interesting is that in the United States this is mentioned more frequently (given that the sample size is small, these data should only be seen as approximate).

The next activity, mentioned by nearly 20% of respondents in each country, is watching already posted videos to find inspiration and to learn. The remaining activities were mentioned by fewer than 10% of those surveyed.

Selected responses are presented below.

I post videos that ensure I will get a high number of viewers (Poland, male, age 30–34).
I watch professional videos that give advice on how to approach various situations (USA, male, age 18–24).
I post videos about myself and things I like (USA, female, age 25–29).

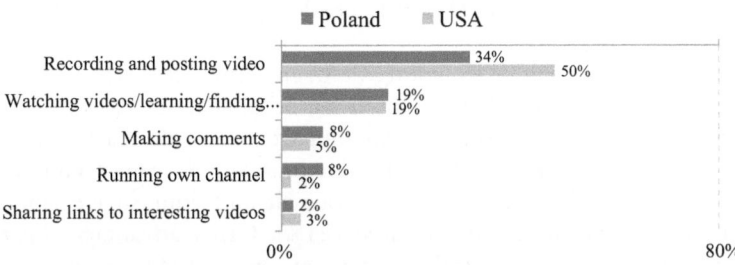

Fig. 5.14 Activities undertaken on YouTube for building a personal brand. Coded answers to open questions ($N = 93$ (Poland); $N = 58$ (USA), individuals building a personal brand, who use YouTube for this purpose. Source: Own research. * The chart shows answers that were given by at least 3% of respondents in at least one country)

Fig. 5.15 Advantages of building a personal brand using YouTube. Coded answers to open questions ($N = 93$ (Poland); $N = 58$ (USA), individuals building a personal brand who use YouTube for this purpose. Source: Own research. * The chart shows answers that were given by at least 3% of respondents in at least one country)

> *I make high-quality videos, for a reason, interesting ones, to attract people to me* (Poland, male, age 18–24).
> *I record myself when I'm creating and post these videos on YouTube* (USA, female, age 18–24).
> *I watch other people's vids* (Poland, female, age 30–34).

As can be seen in Fig. 5.15, young Poles and Americans who create their personal image using YouTube pointed out other advantages of the service. For Poles, the most important advantages were its wide reach (27%) and easy access to interesting content (14%). Americans, however, emphasized how you can use YouTube to show yourself and your strong sides and thereby create the image they desired (21%). Other advantages included wide reach (16%) as well as that videos are an attractive, engaging and contemporary form of communication (16%). The remaining advantages were mentioned by less than 10% of respondents.

Several selected responses are presented below.

> *It gets through to a large number of people* (Poland, male, age 30–34).
> *Millions of users* (USA, male, age 30–34).

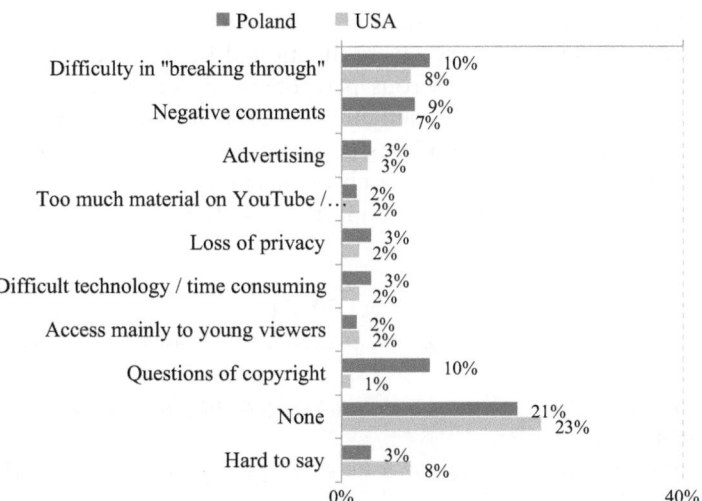

Fig. 5.16 Shortcomings of YouTube as a tool for building a personal brand. Coded answers to open questions ($N = 93$ (Poland); $N = 58$ (USA), individuals building their personal brand, who use YouTube for this purpose. Source: Own research. * The chart shows answers that were given by at least 3% of respondents in at least one country)

You have full control over the vids you post and are sure that they show the image that you're trying to achieve (USA, female, age 25–29).

Free service, wide range of viewers around the world, in various ages and from various cultures, possibility for discussion and seeing opinions beneath materials (Poland, male, age 25–29).

You can show the world who you are, what you like to do and, for example, what talent you have (USA, male, age 25– 29).

Wide selection, showing yourself from a broader, media perspective (Poland, female, age 30–34) (Fig. 5.16).

In response to the question about the shortcomings of YouTube as a tool for creating a personal brand, a significant percentage of respondents (over 20% in each group) answered that it does not have any. Twenty four percent of young Poles and thirty one percent of young Americans mentioned no shortcomings ("none" or "difficult to say"); 10% of Poles and 8% of

Americans mentioned as a shortcoming the difficulty in gaining viewership. Negative comments, "haters", were mentioned by 9% of Poles and 7% of Americans. A relatively numerous percentage of Americans (10%) mentioned problems related to copyright. This problem did not absorb Poles' attention (only 1% of respondents gave such an answer). The remaining shortcomings were mentioned by only a small percentage of those surveyed.

Respondents gave answers about the shortcomings of YouTube as follows:

Low viewership (Poland, male, age 30–34).

The main shortcoming is that the principle of allowable use is not properly followed, and YouTube has a tendency to find you guilty until proven innocent, and will not protect users against false accusations (USA, male, age 25–29).

Exposing yourself to criticism. A lot of competition among wildly different vids (Poland, female, age 30–34).

Unpredictability of the reactions of the potential audience (Poland, male, age 30–34).

Huge volume of other material—needle in a haystack (Poland, female, age 25–29).

There are so many videos that I need to use other social media in order to share mine. Otherwise no one will see them (USA, female, age 25–29).

Reasons for Not Using YouTube for Building a Personal Brand

Individuals who are building their personal image but not using YouTube for that purpose were asked what the reasons were. It should be remembered that all were active users of the service (they used it at least three times a week), and so were competent to make statements regarding the topic (Fig. 5.17).

As can be seen, the fundamental barrier to creating a personal brand on YouTube is the perception of it being too time consuming and technically complicated as well as an inability to record videos or a reluctance to do so.

Respondents made statements on this topic as follows:

I don't want to devote my time to editing a film and other forms I see as ineffective (Poland, female, age 18–24).

Because it requires a video recording, and that is time-consuming (Poland, male, age 18–24).

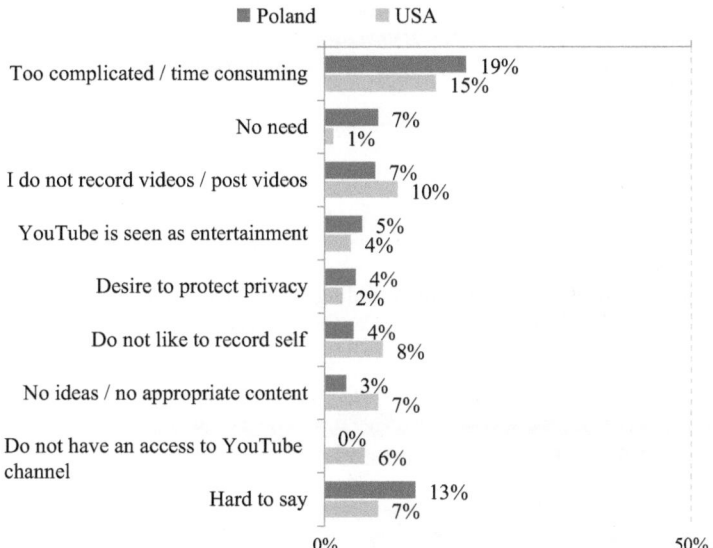

Fig. 5.17 Reasons why young people creating a personal brand do not use YouTube for this purpose. Coded answers to open questions ($N = 233$ (Poland); $N = 163$ (USA), individuals building their personal brand, who do not use YouTube for this purpose. Source: Own research. * The chart shows answers that were given by at least 3% of respondents in at least one country)

> *I don't feel good in front of the camera, I feel it is showing myself too much* (Poland, female, age 18–24).
>
> *I'm not a fan of making videos, I don't have the right abilities. Not that I don't know how to do it, but I don't know what good it would do me to use YouTube for this* (USA, male, age 18–24).
>
> *I'm not very good at videos* (USA, female, age 30–34).
>
> *I'm not a fan of recording yourself* (USA, female, age 25–29).

The Competitive Environment on YouTube in the Context of Creating a Personal Brand

All respondents were asked to create a ranking of the efficacy of social media as tools for creating a personal brand, with the most effective one in first place. Individuals creating a personal brand were requested to respond based on their experience, and those not doing so based on their perception of the media. Of course, the respondents only ranked those media that they knew.

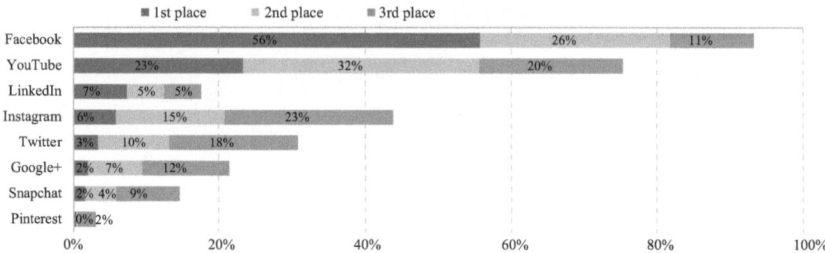

Fig. 5.18 Most effective tools for building a personal brand (ranking), Poland, entire sample ($N = 504$ (Poland). Source: Own research)

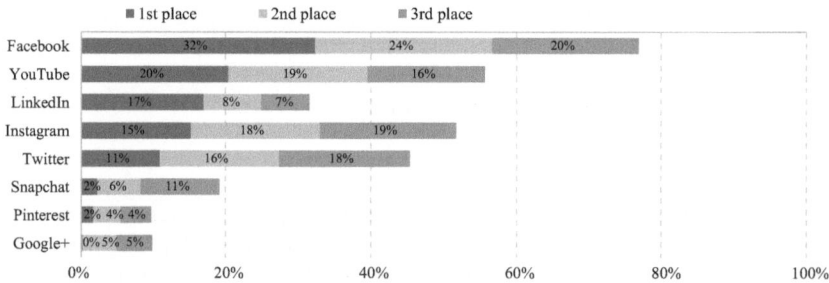

Fig. 5.19 Most effective tools for building a personal brand (ranking), USA, entire sample ($N = 500$ (USA), entire sample. Source: Own research)

In first place in both countries was Facebook (56% Poland, 32% USA); of all social media, it was also most frequently mentioned in the top three (93% of answers in Poland and 77% in the United States).

Second place in terms of the frequency of answers was YouTube: 23% of Poles indicated it as the most effective tool for building a personal brand, and 75% of Poles mentioned it in the top three. Among Americans, these percentages were 20% and 56% respectively. These results show the unquestioned primacy of Facebook, but also the strong position of YouTube as a tool for building a personal brand, as shown in Figs. 5.18 and 5.19.

It should be pointed out that among young respondents in Poland, the medium most frequently indicated was Facebook, and next YouTube, whereby both had a huge advantage over the remaining media, which were chosen as the most effective by less than 10% of those surveyed.

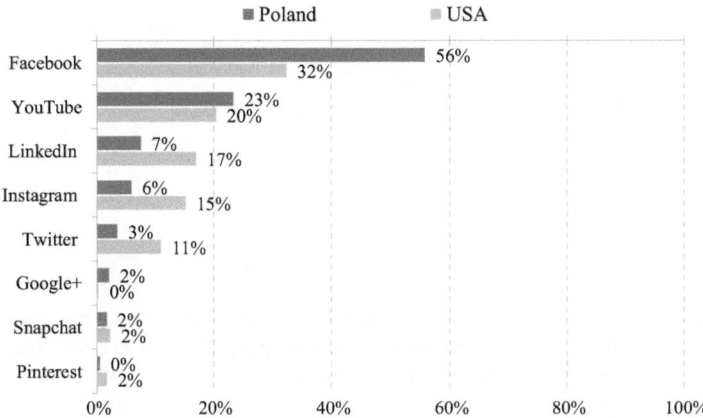

Fig. 5.20 Social media ranked as the most effective for building a personal brand in Poland and the United States ($N = 504$ (Poland); $N = 500$ (USA), entire sample. Source: Own research)

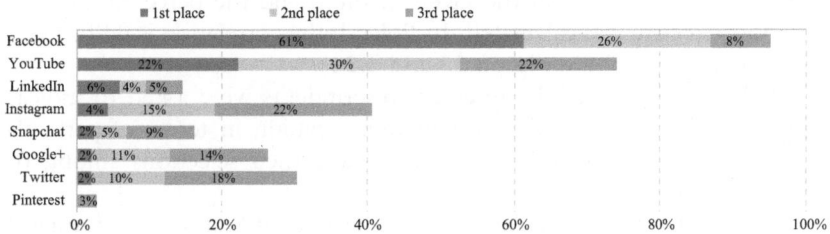

Fig. 5.21 Most effective tools for building a personal brand (ranking), Poland, percent of people consciously creating a personal brand ($N = 310$ (Poland), individuals building a personal brand. Source: Own research)

Among respondents in the United States, the situation is different: Facebook was indeed indicated most frequently (although at a clearly lower level than in Poland), but a significant percentage of those surveyed also mentioned other media as the most effective (Fig. 5.20).

It was also assessed how people creating a personal brand rated social media regarding their efficacy in this regard. It turned out that the perception of the efficacy of social media as a tool for building a personal brand is similar to that seen in the responses given by the entire sample, as illustrated in Figs. 5.21 and 5.22.

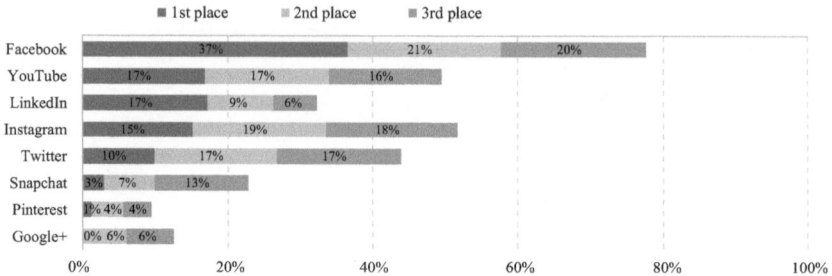

Fig. 5.22 Most effective tools for building a personal brand (ranking), USA, percent of people consciously creating a personal brand ($N = 233$ (USA), individuals building a personal brand. Source: Own research)

As can be seen in the charts, use of a given social media for creation of a personal brand is very strongly correlated with the perception of that medium as the most effective. The analysis was conducted among individuals who are building their personal brand. The Pearson's correlation coefficient between use of the given medium and the perception of it as the most effective was calculated. In Poland, the correlation is 0.96, and in the United States, 0.85 (Figs. 5.23 and 5.24).

At the next stage of the research, respondents were asked to indicate which social medium is the best in their opinion in terms of particular characteristics. Of course, respondents made their selections among the social media they knew.

Respondents both in Poland and in the United States most frequently chose Facebook as the best in terms of all the characteristics indicated in Fig. 5.25. Forty two percent of Poles and thirty percent of Americans indicated Facebook as the tool that stands out for its favorable relationship between time devoted and results produced. Fifty two percent of Poles and thirty three percent of Americans recognized Facebook as the most effective tool, 51% of Poles and 31% of Americans as the tool with the widest reach, and 53% of Poles and 39% of Americans as the best tool in terms of ease of use. Also taking into account the ease of reaching target groups, those surveyed indicated Facebook—55% of Poles and 30% of Americans answered this way.

Among Poles, the most frequent answer in each of these categories was YouTube. Among Americans, YouTube was found in second place in the following categories: efficacy, low costs, wide reach, ease of reaching target

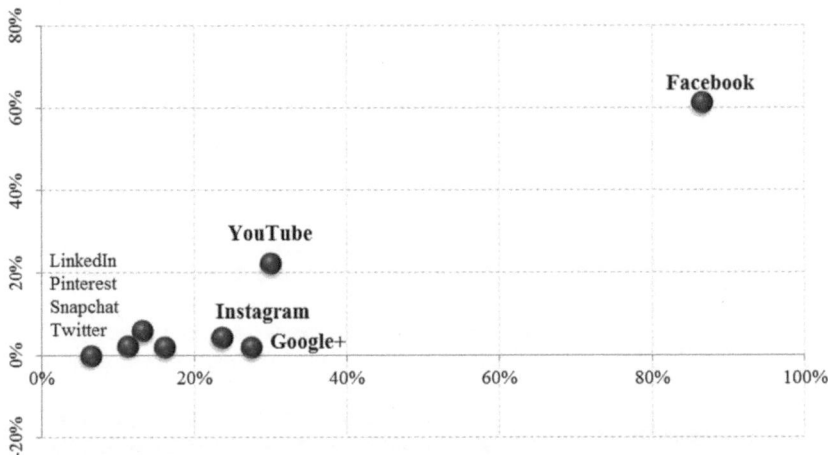

Fig. 5.23 Perception of a given social medium as the most effective for building a personal brand and use of it for this purpose, Poland (X Axis—use of a given medium for building a personal brand. Y Axis—percent of respondents indicating the given medium as the most effective for building a personal brand. $N = 310$ (Poland), individuals building a personal brand. Source: Own research)

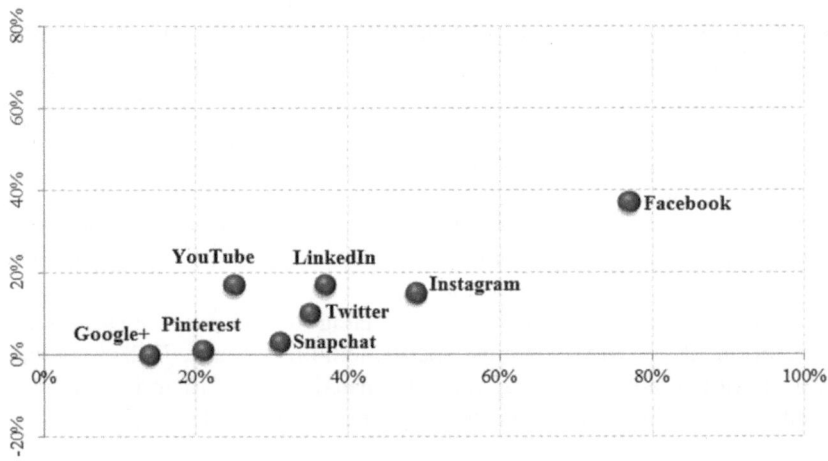

Fig. 5.24 Perception of a given social medium as the most effective for building a personal brand and use of it for this purpose, USA (X Axis—use of a given medium for building a personal brand. Y Axis—percent of respondents indicating the given medium as the most effective for building a personal brand. $N = 233$ (USA), individuals building a personal brand)

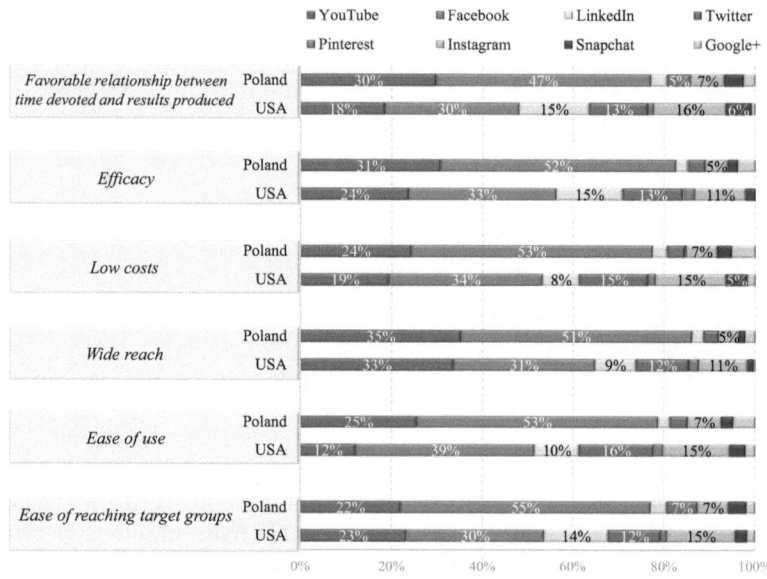

n = 310 (Poland), 233 (USA), individuals building a personal brand
Source: own research.

The chart shows answers that were given by at least 5% of respondents in at least one country

Fig. 5.25 Most effective social media in terms of particular characteristics ($N = 310$ (Poland); $N = 233$ (USA), individuals building a personal brand. Source: Own research)

groups. In the category of ease of use, however, Americans placed Twitter in second place, and shortly behind it, Google+.

There exists a statistically significant correlation between the country of origin of respondents and their choice of the best social medium in terms of the characteristics examined (Table 5.19).

It should be pointed out that an analogous question regarding the perception of the most effective social medium was asked of individuals who do not create a personal brand. It turned out that their answers were similar to those given by those creating a personal brand (Fig. 5.26).

Table 5.19 Correlation between country of origin of respondents and choice of best social medium in terms of all examined characteristics

Statistical tool	Poland vs. USA		
	χ^2	df	p
	Ease of reaching selected groups of receivers		
Pearson's χ^2	53.74055	$df = 7$	$p = 0.00000$
ML χ^2	55.64230	$df = 7$	$p = 0.00000$
	Ease of use		
Pearson's χ^2	68.40118	$df = 7$	$p = 0.00000$
ML χ^2	71.47070	$df = 7$	$p = 0.00000$
	Wide reach		
Pearson's χ^2	52.94561	$df = 7$	$p = 0.00000$
ML χ^2	55.66526	$df = 7$	$p = 0.00000$
	Low costs		
Pearson's χ^2	55.04275	$df = 7$	$p = 0.00000$
ML χ^2	55.86974	$df = 7$	$p = 0.00000$
	Efficacy		
Pearson's χ^2	77.56785	$df = 7$	$p = 0.00000$
ML χ^2	85.30788	$df = 7$	$p = 0.00000$
	Favorable relationship between time devoted and results produced		
Pearson's χ^2	63.74001	$df = 7$	$p = 0.00000$
ML χ^2	65.70417	$df = 7$	$p = 0.00000$

Source: Own research

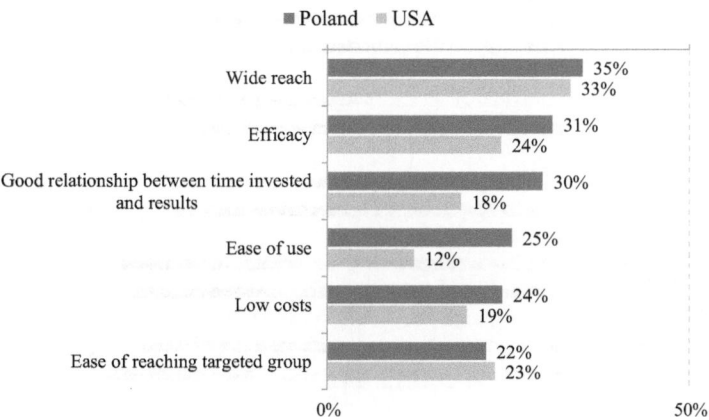

Fig. 5.26 Percentage of respondents indicating YouTube as the most effective social medium in terms of particular characteristics ($N = 310$ (Poland); $N = 233$ (USA), individuals building their personal brand. Source: Own research)

Areas of Life Impacted by a Personal Brand

All respondents were asked to what degree they felt a personal brand could impact a given area of life. A scale of 1–5 was used (1 = no impact at all, 5 = very large impact).

In both countries, the greatest impact was indicated in the area of getting to know new people. Over 40% of young Poles and Americans feel that a good personal brand can have a very large impact on their social life. Somewhat more young people in the United States than in Poland were aware that their personal brand might have a very large impact on getting a job (38% United States, 32% Poland). This may, of course, be associated with the frequent use of LinkedIn, which is a service that is professional in nature (37% of Americans vs. 13% of Poles creating a personal brand use LinkedIn for this purpose). The remaining responses were at a similar level (no significant differences between respondents from both countries).

On this basis, it can be concluded that young people are aware that their personal brand may have an impact on various important elements of their lives. Only a small percentage of respondents believed that a personal brand has no impact at all on various areas of their lives (Fig. 5.27).

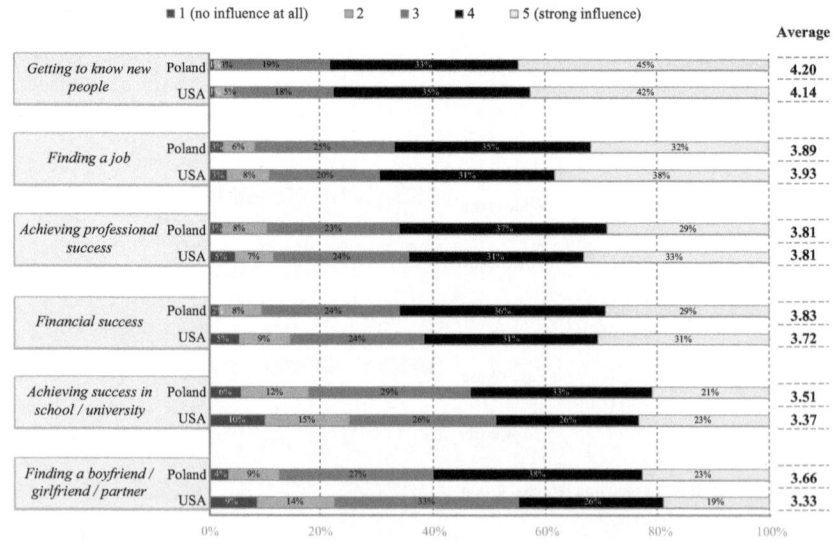

Fig. 5.27 Areas of life that may be impacted by a personal brand (*N* = 504 (Poland); *N* = 500 (USA), entire sample. Source: Own research)

Table 5.20 Correlation between country of origin and the opinion that a personal brand may have an impact on particular areas of life

Statistical tool	Poland vs. USA		
	χ^2	df	p
	Achieving success in professional life		
Pearson's χ^2	6.086457	df = 4	p = 0.19278
ML χ^2	6.109413	df = 4	p = 0.19112
	Achieving success at school/university		
Pearson's χ^2	12.63278	df = 4	p = 0.01322
ML χ^2	12.72365	df = 4	p = 0.01271
	Finding a job		
Pearson's χ^2	8.784493	df = 4	p = 0.06672
ML χ^2	8.802362	df = 4	p = 0.06623
	Getting to know new people		
Pearson's χ^2	5.041797	df = 4	p = 0.28304
ML χ^2	5.126276	df = 4	p = 0.27458
	Finding a boyfriend/girlfriend		
Pearson's χ^2	29.09534	df = 4	p = 0.00001
ML χ^2	29.40447	df = 4	p = 0.00001
	Financial success		
Pearson's χ^2	9.766231	df = 4	p = 0.04456
ML χ^2	9.984077	df = 4	p = 0.04070

Source: Own research

No statistically significant correlation exists between the country of origin of respondents and the opinion that a personal brand may have an impact on the following areas of life: achieving professional success, achieving success in school or university, finding a job and getting to know new people. In contrast, there does exist a statistically significant correlation between the country of origin of participants and the opinion that a personal brand may have an impact on finding a boyfriend, girlfriend or partner, as well as on financial success (Table 5.20).

Individuals who indicated that a personal brand may have a somewhat large or a very large impact on a given area of life were asked to choose the most effective social medium for achieving this goal.

Visible is the primacy of Facebook in the case of goals related to social and emotional life, as well as (in Poland) with finding a job. YouTube, in the view of many respondents (55% in Poland and 39% in the United States) is the best medium for achieving financial success. It has an equally strong

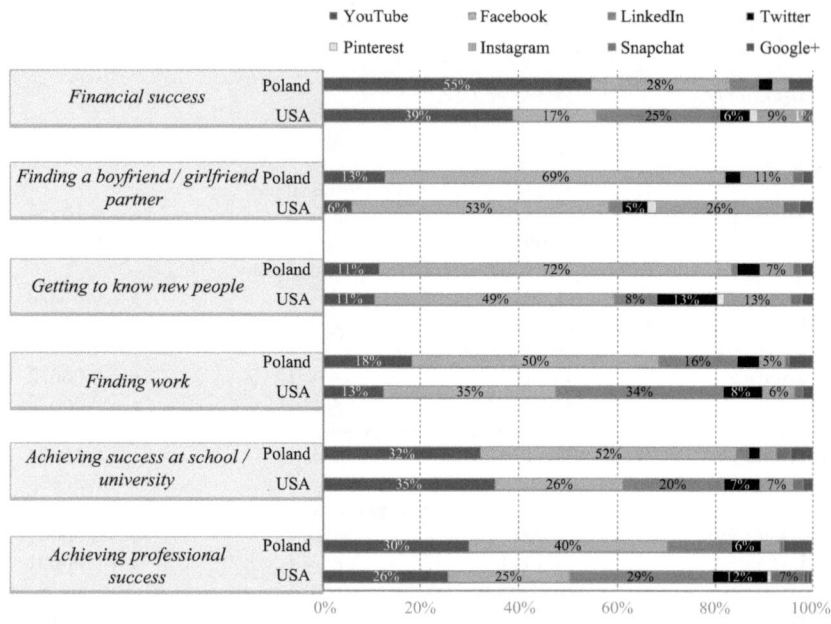

Fig. 5.28 Choice of social medium as best for achieving particular goals (Sample: individuals who feel that a personal brand has an impact on achieving a given goal. Source: Own calculations)

position in such categories as success in school or at university, as well as success in professional life (ca. 30%). Next, LinkedIn has a strong position in the United States as a tool for finding work (34% of responses in the United States), as well as for achieving professional success (29% of responses in the United States). This is clearly associated with the nature of the service (Fig. 5.28).

There exists a statistically significant correlation between the country of origin of respondents and their choice of the best social medium, taking into consideration all of the discussed goals, as Table 5.21 illustrates.

It's interesting how those surveyed perceive YouTube in terms of the goals for which they feel it is most effective in helping to achieve. The strong points of YouTube, in respondents' answers from both countries, are areas associated with financial success and professionalism. It should be mentioned that YouTube is the leader as the medium helping toward financial success (Figs. 5.29 and 5.30).

Table 5.21 Correlation between country of origin of respondents and choice of best social medium in terms of particular goals

Statistical tool	Poland vs. USA		
	χ^2	df	p
	Achieving success in professional life		
Pearson's χ^2	51.80133	$df = 7$	$p = 0.00000$
ML χ^2	53.36634	$df = 7$	$p = 0.00000$
	Achieving success in school/at university		
Pearson's χ^2	71.08669	$df = 7$	$p = 0.00000$
ML χ^2	76.40661	$df = 7$	$p = 0.00000$
	Finding a job		
Pearson's χ^2	41.06237	$df = 7$	$p = 0.00000$
ML χ^2	41.75952	$df = 7$	$p = 0.00000$
	Getting to know new people		
Pearson's χ^2	68.76884	$df = 7$	$p = 0.00000$
ML χ^2	74.83125	$df = 7$	$p = 0.00000$
	Finding a boyfriend/girlfriend		
Pearson's χ^2	44.41973	$df = 7$	$p = 0.00000$
ML χ^2	47.89830	$df = 7$	$p = 0.00000$
	Financial success		
Pearson's χ^2	79.45850	$df = 7$	$p = 0.00000$
ML χ^2	85.12249	$df = 7$	$p = 0.00000$

Source: Own research

Fig. 5.29 Percentage of respondents indicating YouTube as the most effective social medium for achieving particular goals (Source: Own research)

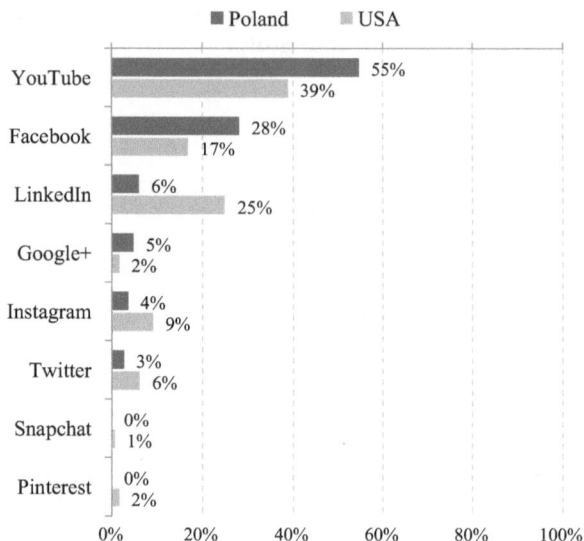

Fig. 5.30   Most effective social media for achieving financial success ($N = 331$ (Poland); $N = 308$ (USA), individuals who believe that a personal brand has a rather large or a very large impact on financial success. Source: Own research)

The data shown in Figs. 5.29 and 5.30 are convergent with the data obtained from the questions regarding awareness of the possibility of earning money from YouTube.

Respondents were also asked whether they know that one can generate revenue through activities on YouTube. Over 80% of respondents in both countries were aware of this. Over one quarter of respondents, both in Poland and in the United States, fully agreed with the statement that activities on YouTube can be a persons' main source of income, as well as that one can earn big money.

Most Effective Media for Building a Personal Brand in the Future

Individuals who declared that they are not building a personal brand were asked whether they plan to begin doing so in the future. Twenty seven percent of respondents in Poland and fifteen percent of respondents in the United States answered that they plan to take up such activities.

Table 5.22   Correlation between country of origin and declared desire to build a personal brand

Statistical tool	Poland vs. USA		
	Plans to build a personal brand		
	χ^2	df	p
Pearson's χ^2	22.16627	$df = 4$	$p = 0.00019$
ML χ^2	22.74297	$df = 4$	$p = 0.00014$

Source: Own research

There exists a statistically significant correlation between the country of origin of respondents and the declaration of a desire to build a personal brand (Table 5.22).

Individuals currently building a personal brand or planning to do so in the future were asked to rank social media in terms of their effectiveness in this area. A time of over the next 2–3 years was given.

Facebook was in first place in both countries (indicated by 47% of respondents in Poland and 33% of respondents in the United States); it was also most frequently indicated in the top three social media (89% in Poland and 75% among respondents in the United States).

YouTube was indicated as first among services by 26% of respondents in Poland and 19% of respondents in the United States. Seventy six percent of those surveyed in Poland and sixty percent of those surveyed in the United States placed it in the top three social media. In the United States, an equally strong position can be seen for LinkedIn (22% of respondents felt that it would be the most effective medium for building a personal brand, 37% chose this medium as one of the three most effective).

Nonetheless, similarly to the case of respondents' evaluation of the current efficacy of social media, these results show the very strong position of Facebook and the strong position of YouTube (Figs. 5.31 and 5.32).

The very strong correlation between perception of a given medium as effective currently and effective in the future is clearly visible. The Pearson's coefficient is 0.98 in Poland and 0.97 in the United States. This is quite understandable, as those surveyed are relying on their experiences and expectations. It is important that they do not see a trend that would

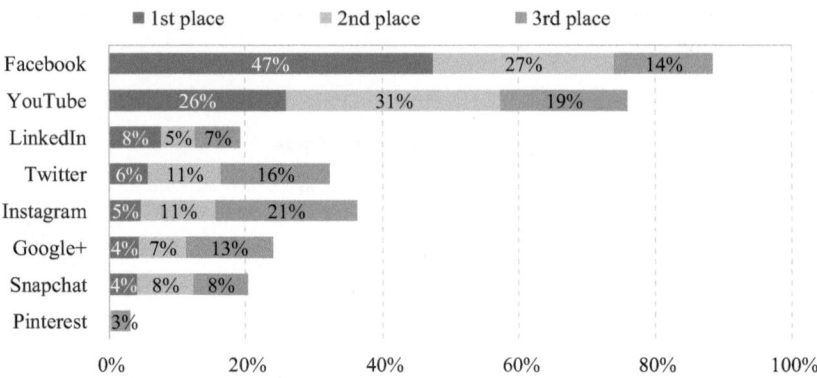

Fig. 5.31 Most effective tool for building a personal brand in the next 2–3 years (ranking), Poland ($N = 365$ (Poland), individuals building a personal brand or planning to begin such activities. Source: Own research)

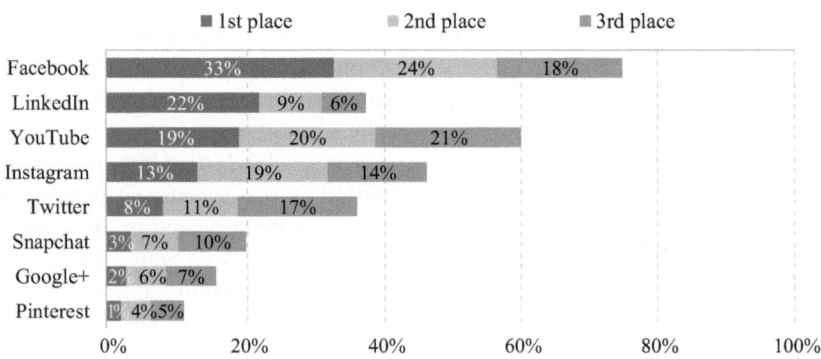

Fig. 5.32 Most effective tool for building a personal brand in the next 2–3 years (ranking), USA ($N = 276$ (USA), individuals building a personal brand or planning to begin such activities. Source: Own research)

significantly change their perspective, although without a doubt the dynamic development and possible changes in the social media market could change these perceptions.

Use and Perception of YouTube

As this work is dedicated to the question of shaping a personal brand using YouTube, it is important how young people use this service and how they perceive it (not necessarily only in the context of shaping a personal brand). Topics related to their attitude toward the service and their interest in subscribing to YouTube channels are particularly interesting. As was shown in the previous chapters, the number of subscribers frequently relates directly to a YouTuber's financial success. In the context of shaping a personal brand, it's also interesting to note what content users most often look for from the service.

Young people were asked to indicate which topics they are interested in on YouTube. These are, above all, entertainment and music (69% in Poland and 76% in the United States). Topics which respondents claimed to be interested in are similar in both countries, with the difference being that young Americans more frequently indicated an interest in games, and young Poles in personal development (Fig. 5.33).

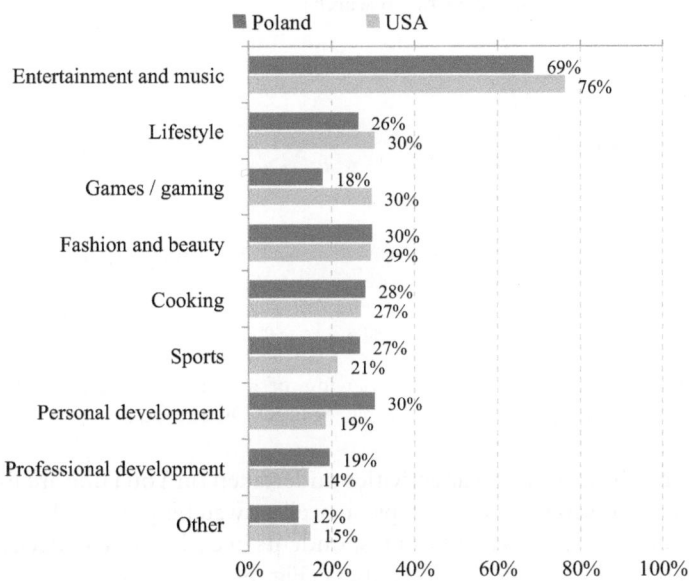

Fig. 5.33 Interest in topics on YouTube ($N = 504$ (Poland); $N = 500$ (USA), entire sample. Source: Own research)

Fig. 5.34 Activities undertaken on YouTube ($N = 504$ (Poland); $N = 500$ (USA), entire sample. Source: Own research)

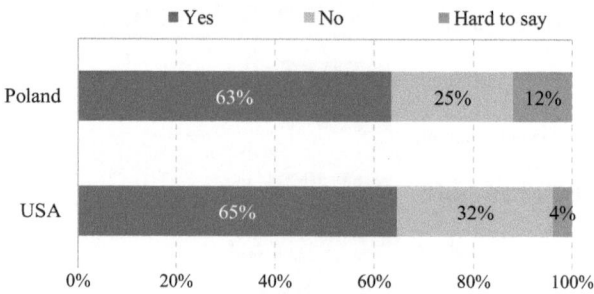

Fig. 5.35 Subscription or regular viewing of a YouTube channel ($N = 504$ (Poland); $N = 500$ (USA), entire sample. Source: Own research)

Among the most popular activities undertaken on YouTube are listening to music and watching video clips, as well as watching films. A significant part of the sample (nearly 60% of respondents in each country) declares that they watch videos made by YouTubers (Fig. 5.34).

A significant part of those surveyed (over 60% in both countries) declare that they regularly watch or subscribe to some channel on YouTube, as illustrated in Fig. 5.35.

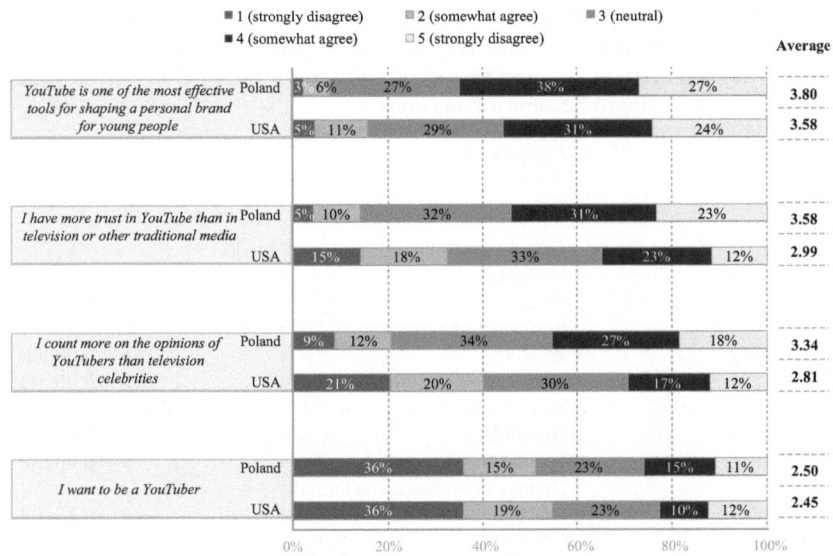

Fig. 5.36 Attitude toward YouTube ($N = 504$ (Poland); $N = 500$ (USA), entire sample. Source: Own research)

It turns out that a significant percentage of young people agree with the statement that YouTube is one of the most effective tools for shaping a personal brand for young people (55% of respondents in the United States, 65% in Poland) (Fig. 5.36). This corresponds to the author's hypotheses that YouTube in particular is one of the most effective tools for shaping a personal brand among members of the young generation. What is important is that only 8% of respondents in Poland and 16% of respondents in the United States do not agree with the statement.

A significant percentage of Poles surveyed declared greater trust in YouTube than in television or traditional media (54% agree with this statement, whereas 15% do not agree). In the case of Americans, such a tendency does not appear. Polish respondents also declared that they rely more on the opinions of known YouTubers than television celebrities (45% agree with this statement, and 21% do not agree). Also in this case, a similar tendency does not appear among respondents from the United States.

Table 5.23 Correlation between country of origin and (1) trust in YouTube compared to traditional media, (2) relying on the opinions of YouTubers, (3) perception of YouTube as an effective tool for shaping a personal brand by young people and (4) desire to become a YouTuber

Statistical tool	Poland vs. USA		
	χ^2	df	p
	Trust in YouTube vs. traditional media		
Pearson's χ^2	63.22803	$df = 4$	$p = 0.00000$
ML χ^2	65.17931	$df = 4$	$p = 0.00000$
	Relying on the opinions of YouTubers vs. TV celebrities		
Pearson's χ^2	49.56437	$df = 4$	$p = 0.00000$
ML χ^2	50.39788	$df = 4$	$p = 0.00000$
	YouTube as an effective tool for shaping a personal brand		
Pearson's χ^2	16.38937	$df = 4$	$p = 0.00254$
ML χ^2	16.58909	$df = 4$	$p = 0.00232$
	Desire to become a YouTuber		
Pearson's χ^2	6.641625	$df = 4$	$p = 0.15608$
ML χ^2	6.671411	$df = 4$	$p = 0.15431$

Source: Own research

Although many young people watch YouTubers, a small portion of those surveyed would like to become one (responding to the statement, "I want to become a YouTuber", fully agree: 11% in Poland, 12% in the United States; fully disagree: 36% in each country).

There exists a statistically significant correlation between the country of origin of respondents and their trust in YouTube compared to traditional media, relying on the opinions of YouTubers, and perceiving YouTube as an effective tool for shaping a personal brand by young people. However, no statistically significant correlation exists between the country of origin of respondents and the desire to become a YouTuber (Table 5.23).

The question regarding monetization of activities on YouTube and financial success was raised during the research in several places on the questionnaire. At one point, those surveyed were asked whether they had heard that it is possible to generate revenue from activity on YouTube. As seen in Fig. 5.37, over 80% of young people are aware of this.

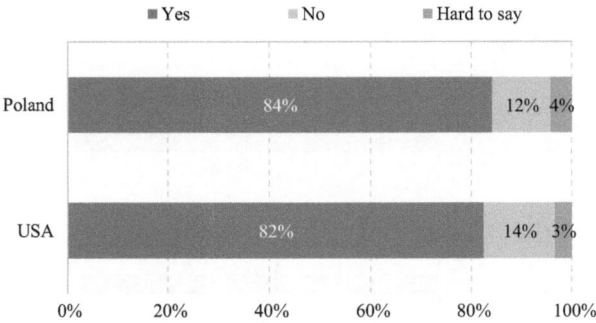

Fig. 5.37 Awareness of the ability to generate revenue through activities on YouTube ($N = 504$ (Poland); $N = 500$ (USA), entire sample. Source: Own research)

Table 5.24 Correlation between country of origin of respondents and awareness of the ability to generate revenue through activities on YouTube

Statistical tool	Poland vs. USA		
	Generation of revenue through YouTube		
	χ^2	df	p
Pearson's χ^2	1.685084	df = 2	p = 0.43061
ML χ^2	1.687423	df = 2	p = 0.43011

Source: Own research

No statistically significant correlation exists between the country of origin of respondents and the awareness of the ability to generate revenue through activities on YouTube (Table 5.24).

Next, the issue of generating revenue from YouTube was examined more deeply and questions asked related to the ability to earn big money from YouTube, seeing YouTube as a primary source of income and as a full-time job. Between 50% and 60% of those surveyed in each country feel that YouTube offers such possibilities (Fig. 5.38).

No statistically significant correlation exists between the country of origin of respondents and their perception of the income potential on YouTube in any of the examined aspects (Table 5.25).

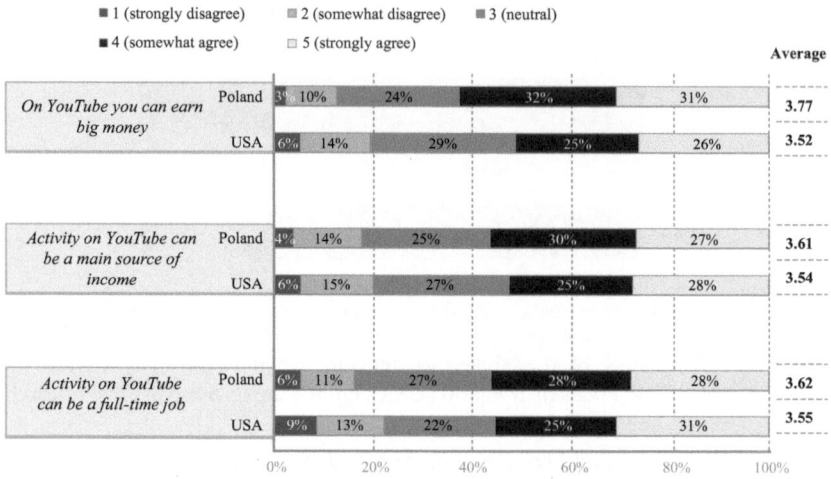

Fig. 5.38 Perception of income potential from YouTube ($N = 504$ (Poland); $N = 500$ (USA), entire sample. Source: Own research)

Table 5.25 Correlation between country of origin of respondents and perception of the income potential from YouTube in all examined aspects

Statistical tool	Poland vs. USA		
	χ^2	df	p
	YouTube—full-time job		
Pearson's χ^2	9.272110	$df = 4$	$p = 0.05465$
ML χ^2	9.313091	$df = 4$	$p = 0.05373$
	YouTube—major source of income		
Pearson's χ^2	3.182039	$df = 4$	$p = 0.52784$
ML χ^2	3.186481	$df = 4$	$p = 0.52712$
	YouTube—big money		
Pearson's χ^2	14.56258	$df = 4$	$p = 0.00570$
ML χ^2	14.64193	$df = 4$	$p = 0.00550$

Source: Own calculations

YouTubers and Social Media Stars

In the research, the topic of YouTubers and social media stars was touched upon as being very important for the question of creating a personal brand. The level of recognizability of YouTubers is an indicator of the efficacy of this social medium in the process of creating a personal brand. In addition, people who observe that others successfully built their personal brands using YouTube may then be more willing to take up this kind of activity, seeing YouTube as an effective tool for building a personal brand.

It therefore seems important that the results showed that respondents declared familiarity with YouTubers who achieved success in this field. A substantial part of the sample (62% in Poland, 69% in the United States) declared that they are aware of YouTubers who built their image using above all the YouTube service (Fig. 5.39).

There exists a statistically significant correlation between the country of origin of respondents and the awareness of a YouTuber who built their image based on YouTube (Table 5.26).

A YouTuber may be—but does not have to be—a social media star. The question of social media stars was also touched upon during the research. Respondents were given the following definition and then asked whether they gather any information on the Internet about stars, and if so, which social media they use for this purpose.

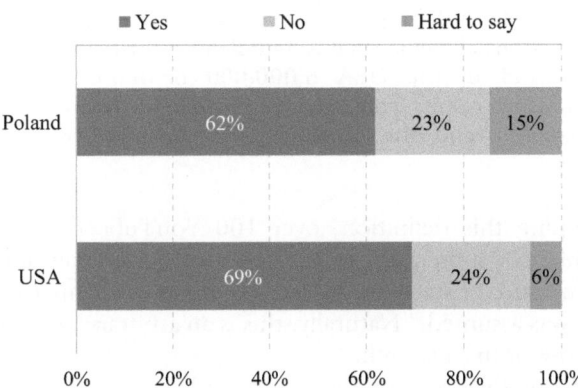

Fig. 5.39 Awareness of a YouTuber who built his/her image based primarily on YouTube ($N = 504$ (Poland); $N = 500$ (USA), entire sample. Source: Own research)

Table 5.26 Correlation between country of origin of respondents and awareness of a YouTuber who built their image on YouTube

Statistical tool	Poland vs. USA		
	Familiarity with a YouTuber		
	χ^2	df	p
Pearson's χ^2	18.52240	$df = 2$	$p = 0.00010$
ML χ^2	18.98832	$df = 2$	$p = 0.00008$

Source: Own research

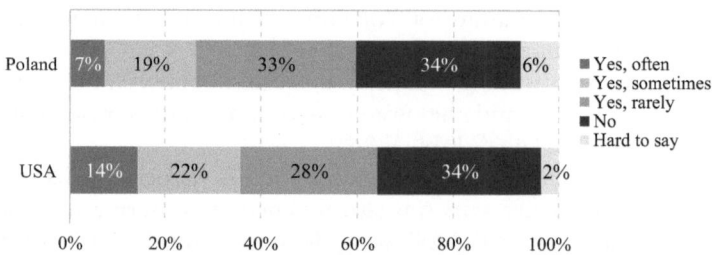

Fig. 5.40 Watching/reading/gathering information on the Internet about social media stars ($N = 504$ (Poland); $N = 500$ (USA), entire sample. Source: Own research)

> A social media star is defined here as someone who has a good number of subscribers on social media (that is, in Poland at least 300,000 YouTube subscribers and in the USA 5,000,000 or more subscribers on YouTube), which results from the differences in the number of residents of each country and the differences in the number of YouTube subscribers.

In developing this definition, over 100 YouTube channels with the highest number of subscribers in each country were taken into consideration. As a measure of stardom, having a number of channel subscribers in the top 100 was assumed.[5] Naturally, this is an arbitrary definition, created for the purpose of this research.

It turned out that 60% of those surveyed in Poland and 64% in the United States look for information about social media stars. Young people in the United States do so more frequently than respondents in Poland (Fig. 5.40).

Table 5.27 Correlation between country of origin of respondents and awareness of social media stars

Statistical tool	Poland vs. USA		
	Awareness of social media stars		
	χ^2	df	p
Pearson's χ^2	26.04955	$df = 4$	$p = 0.00003$
ML χ^2	27.06454	$df = 4$	$p = 0.00002$

Source: Own research

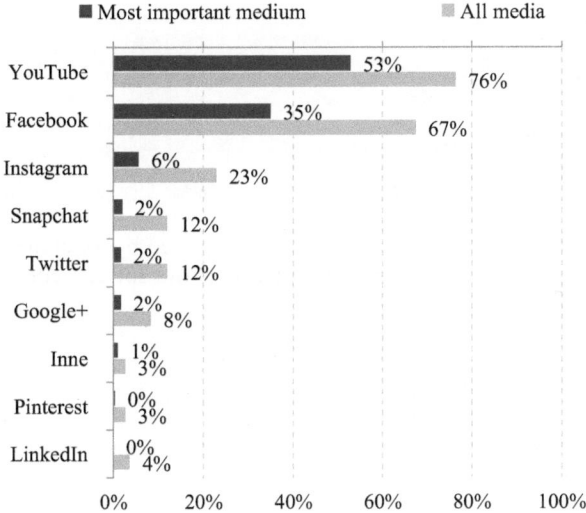

Fig. 5.41 Social media used to receive content placed by social media stars, Poland ($N = 301$, individuals who gather information about social media stars. Source: Own research)

There exists a statistically significant correlation between the country of origin of respondents and their awareness of social media stars (Table 5.27).

In both countries, the most important medium for receiving content placed by social media stars turned out to be YouTube. Among respondents in Poland, it received 53% of responses when asked about the most important medium for receiving such content, and 76% of responses when asked about all media that respondents use to get this content (Figs. 5.41 and 5.42).

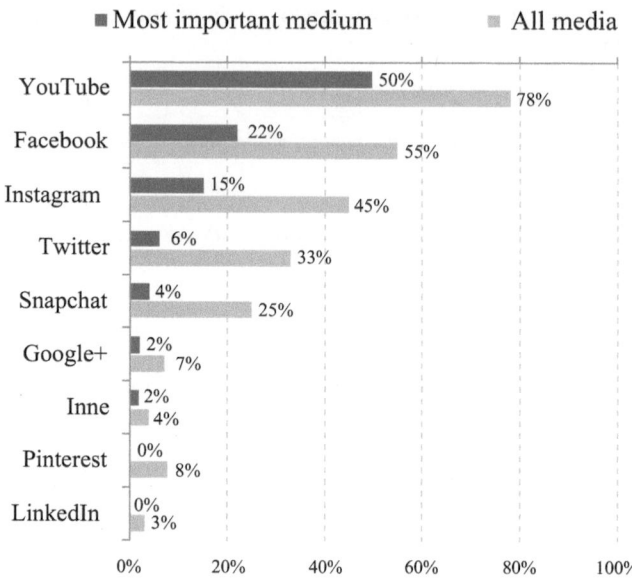

Fig. 5.42   Social media used to receive content placed by social media stars, USA ($N = 321$, individuals who gather information about social media stars. Source: Own research)

Table 5.28 Correlation between country of origin of respondents and use of YouTube to receive content placed by social media stars

Statistical tool	Poland vs. USA		
	YouTube—stars		
	χ^2	df	p
Pearson's χ^2	0.1904434	$df = 1$	$p = 0.66255$
ML χ^2	0.1903770	$df = 1$	$p = 0.66260$

Source: Own research

No statistically significant correlation exists between the country of origin of respondents and the use of YouTube to receive content placed by social media stars (Table 5.28).

NOTES

1. Red Lipstick Monster's statements, as are those of other respondents in both the qualitative and quantitative parts of this chapter, are written in italics, retaining the original style (without language correction).
2. Before working with someone for advertising large brands generally, conduct market research that makes it possible to identify the image of potential brand ambassadors.
3. Translator's note: The Polish original title, *Zrobisz mi loda?*, which is also the question that Wapniak asks strangers in the video, is a clear double-entendre: the sentence can mean either "make me an ice cream?" literally, or unmistakably also "give me a blowjob?"
4. Translator's note: the original, *Potrzymaj moje jajka*, means literally "hold my eggs."
5. Calculated using analytics on socialblade.com

REFERENCES

Bureau of Labor Statistics. (n.d.). Retrieved from http://data.bls.gov/timeseries/LNS14000000

Burnewicz, J. (2007). *Metodologia badań ekonomicznych [lecture summary for doctoral students]*. Gdańsk, Poland: Wydział Ekonomiczny i Wydział Zarządzania Uniwersytetu Gdańskiego.

Central Statistical Office of Poland. (2016, February 22). *Ludność. Stan i struktura ludności oraz ruch naturalny w przekroju terytorialnym.* Stan w dniu 30 VI 2015 r. Retrieved from http://stat.gov.pl/obszary-tematyczne/ludnosc/ludnosc/ludnosc-stan-i-struktura-ludnosci-oraz-ruch-naturalny-w-przekroju-terytorialnym-stan-w-dniu-30-vi-2015-r-,6,18.html

Central Statistical Office of Poland. (n.d.). *Bezrobocie rejestrowane.* Retrieved from http://stat.gov.pl/obszary-tematyczne/rynek-pracy/bezrobocie-rejestrowane

Czakon, W. (2009). Mity o badaniach jakościowych w naukach o zarządzaniu. *Przegląd Organizacji, 9,* 13–18.

Malinowska-Parzydło, J. (2015). *Jesteś marką. Jak odnieść sukces i pozostać sobą.* Gliwice, Poland: One Press.

McNally, D., & Speak, D. K. (2003). *Be your own brand.* San Francisco: Berrett-Koehler Publishers.

Montoya, P., & Vandehey, T. (2005). *The brand called you: The ultimate personal branding handbook to transform anyone into an indispensable brand.* New York: Peter Montoya Publishers.

Rampersad, H. K. (2008). A new blueprint for powerful and authentic personal branding. *Performance Improvement, 6,* 34–37.

Red Lipstick Monster [Grzelakowska-Kostoglu, E.]. (2015a). *About Red Lipstick Monster*. Retrieved from https://www.youtube.com/user/RedLipstickM0nster/about

Red Lipstick Monster [Grzelakowska-Kostoglu, E.]. (2015b). *Red Lipstick Monster. Tajniki makijażu.* Kraków, Poland: Flow Books.

Schawbel, D. (2010). *Me 2.0. 4 steps to building your future.* New York: Kaplan Publishing.

Statistica 10.0 software (StatSoft Inc., 2011).

Szarucki, M. (2010). Metodyka analizy porównawczej w badaniach międzynarodowych. *Zeszyty Naukowe Uniwersytetu Ekonomicznego w Krakowie, 827*, 51–66.

Trzeciak, S. (2015). *Wizerunek publiczny w internecie. Kim jesteś w sieci?* Gliwice, Poland: Helion.

United States Census Bureau. (2014, December 4). *New Census Bureau statistics show how young adults today compare with previous generations in neighborhoods nationwide.* Retrieved from http://www.census.gov/newsroom/press-releases/2014/cb14-219.html

United States Census Bureau. (n.d.). Retrieved from https://www.census.gov/po pest/data/datasets.html

Urban Land Institute. (2015, May 13). *Gen Y and housing: What they want and where they want it.* Retrieved from http://uli.org/report/gen-y-housing-want-want

Wapniak. [Wapiński, M.]. (2015, May 14). *Prank na prezydencie! Wapniak JKM Troll.* Retrieved from https://www.youtube.com/watch?v=HkcXlMZ2W9A

Wojtaszczyk, K., & Maszewski, F. (2014). Różnorodność metod zarządzania marką osobistą. *Prace naukowe Uniwersytetu Ekonomicznego we Wrocławiu, 349*, 454–462.

CHAPTER 6

Research Results, Verification of Research Hypotheses and Recommendations for Practice

Abstract This final chapter offers an interpretation of the results in regard to theory and the current state of the field, and also includes conclusions and recommendations for practice that emerge from the research.

Keywords Research results • Best practices • Branding

FAMILIARITY WITH THE TERM "PERSONAL BRANDING" AND UNDERSTANDING IT SPONTANEOUSLY

The research conducted for this work showed that the recognizability of the term "personal branding" among the study group in Poland is lower than in the group of respondents from the United States. Forty five percent of respondents in Poland recognize the term, and in the United States, 55% of those surveyed do. This suggests that the concept of "personal branding" is closer to American society and, what follows, so too are the practices that constitute it. Here, one can discern an association with the difference in the popularity of key social media. LinkedIn, a social networking service directed toward career development and building professional relationships, is much more popular in the United States than in Poland. This is shown by the research results, according to which LinkedIn is much more popular in the United States than YouTube, while in Poland, it is YouTube that is the

© The Author(s) 2018   169
M. Grzesiak, *Personal Brand Creation in the Digital Age*,
https://doi.org/10.1007/978-3-319-69697-3_6

most popular social medium and LinkedIn has a much lower number of users.

There is a wide range of associations with the term "personal branding" that encompasses many areas of personal and professional activity. At the same time, many people spontaneously speak of creating an appropriate image on social media. It is precisely these social media services that are indicated by respondents as being the most popular locations serving to build a personal brand. They provide many effective tools that make it possible to create one's own image as one wishes. It should be mentioned at this point that 52% of respondents in Poland and 67% of those surveyed in the United states have encountered the term "personal branding" in accordance with the definition presented by the author of this work. Moreover, nearly one quarter of the sample, both in Poland and in the United States declared that they are building their own personal brand in a way that is consistent with the definition provided by the author.

Awareness of Building a Personal Brand

The research results also show that a relatively high number of those studied engage in activities to build their brand without being aware that these are in fact personal branding activities. This was revealed by the research conducted by the author—this behavior was declared by as many as 40% of the studied group from Poland and 24% of respondents from the United States. This indicates that in the United States, a far greater number of people are aware in what way and with which tools and actions they can build a personal brand. In the case of those surveyed in Poland, a high percentage of those studied undertake certain actions unconsciously, unaware that they are, in effect, creating a personal brand. This lack of awareness may cause such unorganized and unconscious activity to negatively effect their personal brand. This explains many of the behaviors of Polish users of social media, who, for example, post compromising photos or video material, which has the effect of making employers less inclined to hire them.

Goal of Building a Personal Brand

Among the most important goals of building a personal brand, two can be highlighted. The first of these is the need to create a positive image, thanks to which individuals creating a personal brand will be perceived favorably in their environment. They will achieve and maintain the desired (positive) image among those who know them, both in the real world and on the Internet. The second fundamental goal of building a personal brand is to achieve success in professional life. Those surveyed declared that appropriate building of a personal brand is directly linked with career development. They also state that a well-created personal brand can make it easier to receive a promotion or better job offers, which translates into a higher level of income.

Ways of Building a Personal Brand

According to respondents, the best way to build a personal brand is to be active on social media, understood as regularly posting texts, photos and video materials. Both among respondents in the United States and those surveyed in Poland, the most frequently used medium for this purpose is Facebook. Among those who declared that they were creating a personal brand, as many as 86% of respondents in Poland and 77% of those surveyed in the United States use this service. The proportions turn out differently in the case of YouTube, which is used for creation of a personal brand by 30% of respondents in Poland and 25% of those surveyed in the United States. Among the Polish respondents, YouTube is in second place in the ranking of services used to create a personal brand, whereas among those surveyed in the United States, it was in sixth place (after services such as Instagram, LinkedIn, Twitter and Snapchat).

The situation is similar in the case of the assessment of the efficacy of social networking services for the creation of a personal brand. In the ranking of social media in this regard, the winner is also Facebook, which was indicated as the most effective tool by 56% of Poles and 32% of Americans studied. YouTube was identified as the most effective tool for building a personal brand by 20% of respondents in both countries.

Assessment of YouTube as a Tool for Creating a Personal Brand

The research shows that the main activity undertaken on YouTube for building a personal brand is making and posting videos. It turns out, however, that a significant percentage of those studied (ca. 19% in the groups from each country) use it as a source of knowledge and inspiration.

An advantage of YouTube in this area is its wide, international reach (mentioned by 27% of respondents in Poland and 16% of those surveyed in the United States, who declared that they are creating a brand on YouTube), as well as the ability to show one's strong sides (21% of Americans surveyed), and the fact that videos are an attractive and contemporary form of communication (16% of Americans studied).

In addition, YouTube was indicated by respondents as a place where one can achieve financial success. Many of those studied stated that professional management of a YouTube channel, after achieving an appropriate reach and viewership is a tool for generating profits. Income can flow from advertising or from promotional work for commercial brands. YouTube was equally valued as a place to construct one's professional image, but also as a medium through which one can achieve success at school or university. Over 80% of respondents in Poland and in the United States are aware that by being active on YouTube one can earn income. Between 50% and 60% of those studied in each country agree with the statement that one can earn big money on YouTube. Taking into consideration these declarations by respondents, as well as the strong position of YouTube in regard to the perceived opportunities for income, we can expect a growing role of this service as a tool for creating a personal brand among young people.

YouTubers and Social Media Stars

A significant proportion of those studied in each country (62% in Poland, 69% in the United States) recognize and are familiar with at least one YouTuber who built their image working, above all, on the YouTube service. A similar percentage of young people seek information about social media stars, and YouTube is the main medium for delivery of the content that they create.

Fundamental Differences Between Young Poles and Americans in the Area of Creating a Personal Brand

The research made it possible to identify important differences between respondents in the United States and Poland regarding the instruments and activities serving to create a personal brand. First, the Americans studied were substantially more frequently familiar with the term "personal branding" than those Poles surveyed. Second, the differences were also evident with regard to the conscious creation of a personal brand. A significantly higher percentage of Poles studied than Americans studied created their personal brand unconsciously (40% vs. 24%). Unconscious, meaning here that they undertake activities that de facto create a personal brand, but presumably without the knowledge that these actions have particular consequences. Third, the activities of the Americans studied in the area of creating a personal brand were quite diverse: in this process, they used more social media (on average 2.9, while Poles researched use on average 2.1). Among respondents in the United States, decidedly more popular than among those surveyed in Poland were social media services like Instagram, LinkedIn, Twitter, Snapchat and Pinterest. Among Polish respondents, however, Google+ was more popular. And finally: it also seems that Americans creating a personal brand place more emphasis on questions related to professional success than do Poles. The Americans studied used LinkedIn more frequently than Poles (37% vs. 13%), and in their answers to open questions they spoke about achieving business goals, promotions, employment and networking.

CATALOG OF GOOD PRACTICES

The conclusions that arise from the research conducted as well as the topic area of this work allow formulation of a list of behaviors, activities and attributes that condition the attainment of maximum efficacy in building a personal brand using YouTube. This is presented below.

Interactivity

It is important to maintain constant contact with viewers of one's YouTube channel by reacting to their needs and questions expressed in comments. Another good practice is to engage in discussion with subscribers even in situations when they express criticism of the quality of content of the channel, as well as tailoring the content so that it meets the concrete expectations of viewers to a maximum possible degree.

Cooperation with Other YouTubers

One should take up collaborative work with other YouTubers such as recording video material or taking part in the same promotional activities in order to expand one's reach and the recognizability of the channel, to draw the attention of users and the subscribers of the person invited to cooperate.

Format Predictability

It is important to tailor the form of the content in such a way that it will be predictable for subscribers, clearly defined and will fit well into one of the well-recognized channel formats. Thanks to this, viewers will always know what content or form they can expect in the posted materials. This predictability makes it easier for users to make decisions regarding subscriptions and to view the given channel regularly.

Consistency

It is recommended to regularly post new content, always at the same time in a particular cycle, for example once a week on Monday at 5:00 p.m. Inconsistency in the posted content, whether in terms of its regularity or its cyclical nature, causes a loss of users and a reduction in the number of subscribers.

Unique Personality

Another useful technique is creating and consistently using a unique personality that not only can be easily remembered by users, but also easily distinguished from others creating a personal brand. A unique personality is most often created by a certain choice of clothing, a distinctive use of language (including elements of body language), as well as the way of communicating. The more precisely and consistently the personality presented in video materials is constructed, the easier it will be remembered by users and distinguished from others.

Multi-Channel Presence

Being present in and using the communication possibilities of other social media (such as Facebook, Instagram, Snapchat or LinkedIn) by publishing content with references to one's YouTube channel increases the reach of communication and attracts the interest of users outside of YouTube.

Tailored Target Group

Another important factor is precisely defining the target group for content, in terms of both its demographic and psychographic profile as well as constructing in this way the forms and contents of a message, so that it addresses the needs of that group to a maximum possible degree. Any communication not taking this into consideration provokes conflict on the side of the receiver and a sense of uncertainty regarding his or her status as the appropriate recipient of the communication.

Working with Brands

Taking up cooperation with brands, both in the area of advertising (by including advertising for brands on one's channel or through product placement), and in reviewing (by evaluating specific products provided by producers), on the one hand makes it possible to earn income, and on the other increases the reach of the channel to new groups of recipients.

Product Sales

One can take advantage of the popularity and recognizability of a channel to sell one's own products which bear advertising for the same channel, such as mugs, t-shirts and other types of gadgets.

Media Publications

Promotion of the activity of the channel through media relations, through press releases providing information regarding the existence of the channel, its goals and the content posted on it is also important. This is a way to cultivate a media presence and the interest of journalists in one's work, in order to use press information to grow the recognizability of the channel.

Book Publications

After one has assembled the necessary amount of content one can compile that of the greatest value for users and publish it in book form at one's own cost or with the participation of a proper publisher, which assures an additional form of promotion. A book publication raises the reputation of a channel and is a very important reinforcement of the value of the personal brand in the eyes of users.

Meetings with Users

Taking part in mass events is an excellent platform for making contacts and meetings between YouTubers and their fans. This provides the opportunity to expand the recognizability of the channel, to promote it and to gain new users and subscribers.

SUMMARY

This research without a doubt indicates that the hypothesis that YouTube is one of the most effective tools for shaping a personal brand among members of the young generation was positively verified. In this respect, it takes second place, after Facebook, both among Americans studied and among Polish respondents.

YouTube is seen as the best for achieving financial success—55% of Poles studied and 39% of Americans studied think so. Moreover, they indicate that this tendency will continue, namely, that in the next 2–3 years YouTube will be used by people wanting to build a personal brand or planning to take up such activities (so declare 26% of Poles and 22% of American studied). Among declared activities on YouTube, watching materials posted by YouTubers is in third place—57% of Poles studied and 56% of Americans surveyed do so, which indicates the efficacy of this service as a tool for building a personal brand.

Sixty five percent of Poles and fifty five percent of Americans agree with the statement that YouTube is the most effective tool for building a personal brand by young people. Moreover, 84% of surveyed Poles and 82% of Americans studied are aware that one can earn income through activity on YouTube.

Around two thirds of those studied (62% of Poles and 69% of Americans) declare familiarity with a YouTuber, building an image by the skillful use of YouTube. Among respondents taking part in the research, 59% of Poles and 64% of Americans watch social media stars on the Internet, read about them or seek information about them. YouTube is the social medium most frequently used to receive content posted by social media stars—use of YouTube for this purpose is declared by 76% of Poles surveyed and 78% of Americans studied.

All these data indicate an increasing importance of YouTube in the process of shaping a personal brand and indicate that this service creates enormous opportunities in this area. What is important is that many people are aware of the role that YouTube plays in shaping a personal brand and even declare a desire to take the opportunities provided by this service. In the view of those surveyed, presence on YouTube and creation of a personal brand using it are clearly linked with the possibility of achieving financial success and building one's own recognizability.

This work constitutes only an introduction into further explorations of the important medium that YouTube is today and will be in the future. The author would like to express the hope that it may be an inspiration for further studies. It would be particularly interesting to conduct a detailed study of the relation between the time needed to shape a professional personal brand and earning a basic personal income, or also the growth in interest by firms and organizations in the shaping of brands and earning income from these activities. The research field appears to be quite wide, and the results of potential studies could contribute significantly to the understanding of trends and changes in the means for promotion and distribution of content using social media like YouTube.

INDEX

Note: Page number followed by 'n' refer to notes.

© The Author(s) 2018
M. Grzesiak, *Personal Brand Creation in the Digital Age*,
https://doi.org/10.1007/978-3-319-69697-3